With

THE BOYS

◇◇◇◇◇

Jake MacDonald

WITH THE

| | | | | | | | | | | | | | | | | | | | | | | | | | | | | | | | | | | | | | | | | | | | | | | | | | | | |

Boys

FIELD NOTES ON BEING A GUY

GREYSTONE BOOKS

Douglas & McIntyre Publishing Group
Vancouver/Toronto/Berkeley

| | | | | | | | | | | | | | | | | | | | | | | | | | | | | | | | | | | | | | | | | | | | | | | | | | | | |

Greystone Books
A division of Douglas & McIntyre Ltd.
2323 Quebec Street, Suite 201
Vancouver, British Columbia
Canada V5T 2S7
www.greystonebooks.com

Library and Archives Canada Cataloguing in Publication
MacDonald, Jake, 1949–
With the boys : field notes on being a guy / Jake MacDonald.

ISBN-13 978-1-55365-066-9   ISBN-10 1-55365-066-2

1. Outdoor recreation—Anecdotes.
2. Male friendship—Anecdotes. 3. MacDonald, Jake, 1949– —Anecdotes.
4. MacDonald, Jake, 1949– —Travel. I. Title.
HQ1090.M28 2005   799'.081   C2005-900020-1

Library of Congress information is available upon request.

Earlier versions of some of these pieces have appeared in
Outdoor Canada, Explore, and *Sporting Classics.*

Editing by Barbara Pulling
Copy-editing by John Eerkes-Medrano
Cover and text design by Peter Cocking
Cover photograph by Alexander Walter/Getty Images
Printed and bound in Canada by Friesens
Printed on acid-free paper that is forest friendly
(100% post-consumer recycled paper) and has been processed chlorine free
Distributed in the U.S. by Publishers Group West

We gratefully acknowledge the financial support of the Canada
Council for the Arts, the British Columbia Arts Council, and
the Government of Canada through the Book Publishing Industry
Development Program (BPIDP) for our publishing activities.

For my father,

Donald Ian MacDonald,

October 4, 1913–October 13, 2001

||||||||||||||||||||||||||||||||||||||||||||||||

CONTENTS

With
THE BOYS

◇◇◇◇◇

II

INTRODUCTION

The stories in this book cover a period of approximately forty years. Some of the early events took place before I became a writer, so these are recollections, and I couldn't testify in court as to their factuality. It's a trick of memory that we tend to revise the details of our past. And it's a trick of the eye that when we're trying to spot something, like a faint star, we can see it more clearly when we look off to one side. So these are sidelong dispatches, field notes taken during my travels with fathers and sons, relatives and buddies. If the stories reveal anything about men's lives, I'm pleased. But they're intended to be stories, not lessons. If they seem to have a moral, I'm afraid it's purely accidental.

Women appear in some of the stories too. Even when they're not on the scene, their absence is a kind of presence. Women keep an eye on men and exert a moderating influence on their behavior. That's one of the reasons that men like to occasionally get away from them. The singer Garth Brooks once remarked that he was teaching his little daughters a simple concept: "Men are pigs." All men know this about themselves, and they think it's funny. But at the same time, they have their own gender-specific code of ethics. Some kinds of piggy behavior are allowed, and some aren't. There are hundreds of rules affecting male behavior. That's too many to list here, and in any case every guy knows them. But women might find the male codebook strange and interesting. Women, for example, commonly assume that men like to talk about their spouses or sweethearts with their buddies. This is what psychologists call "projection." Women do it, so they think men do it too. A woman will happily dump the entire kitbag of her romantic woes on the table for the amusement of some other woman she's met four minutes ago. But no matter how late the evening or how debauched the conversation, you'll seldom hear a man say more than a few neutral words in passing about his mate. In the male codebook, talking about your love life is considered to be craven and unmanly. So women can at least relax about that.

Some of these stories have a wide cast of characters. Like most men, I seem to belong to various male groups that come together for seasonal banquets, fishing derbies, snooker tournaments, and what have you. The anthropologist Lionel Tiger says the phenomenon of club membership is an aspect of the "male hunting bond." He says that men have an instinctive need to assemble, invent uniforms, devise rites of passage, and go after arbitrary goals of some kind, often with surrogate weapons like golf clubs or pool cues or hockey sticks. As the first story in the collection explains, my father belonged to a hunting group, and he drafted me at an early age. He and his friends taught me a lot of things. They offered these lessons in an indirect sort of way that made me feel I was learning

2

rather than being taught: a subtle distinction, but one that makes a big difference to a boy. They didn't just teach me about hunting, either. We could have been sailing a ship or building a barn, and the lessons would have been the same.

My father and his cronies are long gone. But every October, I still assemble with a group of friends for a weeklong waterfowl hunt in western Manitoba. I don't know if we're a great example of the hunting bond, because we honestly don't care much about competition. What draws us together is friendship, relaxation, and the sheer physicality of the hunt, the pleasure of getting muddy, getting hungry and honestly tired in the golden fields of autumn. A century or two ago, Western civilization moved indoors, and it's a marvel to go back outside for a week and reclaim the life of vigor. In the darkness of early morning, knee-deep in icy water, sitting on a muskrat house, watching the stars fade, watching the eastern sky turn pink while invisible wings whistle overhead, you'd have to be a lawyer like Atticus Finch at his eloquent best to convince us that at this particular moment we're not making better use of the morning than anyone else on the continent.

My gal Ann—who supports the tradition of males (and females) in groups—thinks we assemble with old friends to weave a line of continuity into our lives. For eighteen years, she and her friends have gathered every month for their book club. Divorce, disaster, and personal tragedy have marked their journey, but the book club forges on. I have a daughter, and she and her friends do much the same thing. "I want everything to stop changing," Caitlin once said to me when she was five years old, holding my hand, standing on a sidewalk looking at our neighborhood grocery store with an OUT OF BUSINESS sign on the front door. That store had been one of our landmarks. She knew the butcher, she knew the lady at the cash register, and she was heartsick to see that the

3

store was gone and was never coming back. Caitlin is twenty years old now, and she has her own close-knit group of girl-friends, whose devotion to one another is a fixed waypoint in a world that never stops changing. "We don't care about boys anymore," she says. "Boys come and go, but your friends are always there. When we go out on Friday night, we just laugh and laugh. Honestly, Dad, I can't tell you how much fun we have."

While I'm on the subject of friends, I should explain to my own crew that certain individuals, like Steve Alsip and Charles Wilkins, get their own stories in this collection not because they deserve it any more than you do, but because we undertook some interesting journeys together. If you're not in this book, you'll be in the next one. Some of the stories are about friends I never knew: Ernest Hemingway, for example, who died in 1961 but nevertheless seems to be a daily presence in my life. A few years ago I noticed that it was difficult if not impossible to get through a normal day of reading the paper, browsing the *New Yorker,* going for lunch, surfing the net, and listening to CBC Radio without encountering the H word. For some reason Hemingway's name seems to have become stuck, like the line of a skipping record, inside the language of the mass media. Advertising campaigns have even linked cigar brands, restaurants, and styles of clothing with his name. (Hemingway wore khaki!) Can anyone explain this? It can't be his literary influence. After all, when was the last time anyone told you they were halfway through a Hemingway novel?

On first noticing this phenomenon, I wondered if it had sprung out of my own preoccupations. I mentioned it to a female friend, the late Carol Shields, and she thought I must be imagining it. Then a few months later, during one of our periodic lunches, she reported that she'd conducted the same experiment and confirmed that it was true. I admire many of

4

Hemingway's books, but I confess to some ambivalence about the long shadow he throws across modern literature. Reviewers tend to wheel out the н word whenever they see someone fishing or hunting inside the covers of a book, and for some reason critics also regard large portions of Spain, Paris, Michigan, Idaho, the Florida Keys, the Bahamas, and Cuba as his literary turf—"Hemingway country." A few years ago the writer Paul Quarrington and I headed down to the island of Bimini, one of Papa's old haunts, to do some fishing and see what we could learn about the strange, almost Marilyn Monroe–like endurance of the Hemingway myth.

Some of the characters in these stories are no longer alive. One of my oldest friends, Bob Murray, had a son named Blair. My daughter and I went to Disney World about ten years ago with Bob and his family. Blair seemed like a bright and happy kid. I can still see him running on the beach at Cape Canaveral. Every year, Bob and Blair came on our annual hunting trip to western Manitoba. Two years ago, Blair went home after the hunt and killed himself. Two other members of our group, Kerry Dennehy and Ken Powell, have lost their sons to suicide, and they've done their best to show Bob that he's not alone.

The dead stay with us, in their invisible way. And as we grow older their number grows. Every spring I attend a large, fairly dressy, all-male wild-game dinner at our local squash and racket club. It's called the Passwa Dinner, and you have to be inducted to attend. There are some funny speeches, some of them by old-timers who looked the devil in the face in Normandy and other places, and there's usually an informative lecture by a guest speaker. (Last year it was a scientist who told us all about brain diseases in white-tailed deer.) Dinner consists of caribou, arctic char, moose, and other delicacies that the members have donated. One of the rituals of the evening is to raise a glass to absent friends, and with a moment of silence to send our thoughts to our departed, wherever they are.

We all have our names in the program, and if you have an asterisk beside your name it means you're a ghost. Two years ago it was white-haired, loud-voiced old Gerry Dennehy who won the asterisk. We saluted Gerry (Kerry's dad) at the dinner, and at the request of Dodie, his widow, we took him along on our fall hunting trip, in a plastic bag. At the tailgate lunch we raised a glass, observed a moment of silence, and honored him with a twenty-one-shotgun salute. A few days later, when the boys were pushing their way across a field of cut sunflowers and the afternoon sun was throwing the poignant warmth of late October, Gerry's son Shaun decided it was time. He opened the big plastic sack and broadcast his father's ashes into the wind.

Shaun had always been one of the main organizers of the hunt. He lived in Whitehorse, Yukon, and often got in touch with the rest of us by telephone months ahead of time, making sure everyone had the week blocked off on their calendar. Last year, a month or so before the hunt, Shaun was working on his computer late at night when the power went off. Since he had bone cancer, he was reluctant to get up and try to find his way around in the dark. So he waited and waited. Finally, he decided to take a chance. He got up, tripped on something, fell hard, and shattered his pelvis. In his customary deadpan voice, calling me from his hospital bed, he added: "What really pissed me off was as soon as I hit the floor the power came back on." The damage was irreparable. The pain was so severe that the doctors had frozen his lower body with a spinal sedative. Shaun couldn't come on the hunt, but he sent his son Quinn to represent him.

Quinn is a slender, dark-haired thirteen-year-old with his mother's good looks and his father's habit of thinking instead

6

of talking. When Shaun drove his old Suburban down a dirt road, you'd see Quinn hanging his head out the back window like a dog, his hair flipping in the breeze as he stared down at the ground rolling by. Quinn hunted with his uncle Kerry, and they phoned Shaun to give him the dailies. One sunny afternoon at the tailgate lunch, we called Shaun on a cell phone and told him Quinn had bagged a nice Canada goose that very morning. He was glad to hear our reports. Was the weather holding? Were there any grouse around? Shaun liked nothing more than walking for miles along the hedgerows looking for sharp-tailed grouse, and he was pleased that we'd visited some of his favorite spots and picked up a few. At the end of the week, Quinn flew back home. And Shaun, as though he'd been waiting, died a few days later.

Where did he go? It's the eternal question. About fourteen centuries ago, an Italian missionary named Paulinus visited Northumbria, England, and met with a group of English warlords. At this meeting, one of the lords stood up and made a speech, in which he compared human existence to a feast that takes place in a great meeting hall in wintertime. "There is a fire burning on the hearth in the middle of the hall, while outside the wintry storms of rain and snow are raging—and a sparrow flies swiftly through the hall. It enters in at one door and quickly flies out through the other. For the few moments it is inside, the storm and wintry tempest cannot touch it, but after the briefest moment of calm, it flits from your sight, out of the wintry storm and into it again. So this life of man appears but for a moment. What follows or, indeed, what went before, we know not at all."

Next year, Quinn will return for the hunt. He's been washed in the blood and is now a member. And at some point, when the time seems right, we'll honor Shaun. We'll raise our glasses, fire a salute, and then we'll carry on.

7

The

COMMISSIONER

◇◇◇◇◇

*I*n the television series Batman there was a character known as Commissioner Gordon. I never understood exactly what Commissioner Gordon did for a living, but whatever he did, my father did the same thing. My father was the commissioner of Metropolitan Winnipeg. When my friends asked me about his occupation, I said, "He's like Commissioner Gordon on Batman," and that seemed to satisfy them.

Unlike the silvery-haired buffoon on the TV show, my father was a stand-up guy, an unpretentious and no-nonsense fellow who often wore his beat-up parka to the office and received friendly waves from janitors, street cops, firemen, and his other employees at City Hall. His common-man style was deliberate. Educated in economics at the University of Toronto, he was what social commentators used to call a "Roosevelt liberal," a believer in good government and a champion of the underdog.

9

My father loved the world of nature, and he loved birds most of all. At his summer cottage at Lulu Lake, in northwestern Ontario, he put homemade birdhouses in each tree. On summer days, blackbirds, warblers, jays, swallows, and flycatchers darted through the foliage and filled the air with a wild partying chatter. My father's favorite birds were ducks and geese. He had paintings of exotic ducks on the walls of the cottage, and the bookshelf at home was filled with massive textbooks and coffee table books about waterfowl.

He also loved hunting. Every fall, "Mac" (as my mother called him) went duck hunting for four or five weekends with his friends in the marshes of western Manitoba. I know that some people might find it hard to understand how a man who loved birds could also take pleasure in hunting them. Those were the days before political correctness, before one's automobile, hobbies, and even dietary habits were considered "statements," and I don't think it ever crossed my dad's mind that what he did in his spare time was anyone's damn business. My mother is the sort of person who will go to some lengths to capture a bumblebee in a jar rather than swat it with a newspaper, so I don't know what she thought of the bird-hunting issue. But she seemed to accept it, as part of his gruff outdoorsy style. My dad never explained why he hunted, or why he wanted me, his eldest son, to accompany him, but I think he had some kind of silent conviction that the rituals of the hunt would teach me something.

So every Thursday afternoon in October we'd load the family's big white 1959 Buick with wonderfully masculine stuff—sleeping bags, chest waders, boots, duck decoys, whisky, coolers stuffed with steaks, garlic sausage, stinky cheeses, and Black Label beer, guns, ammunition, and of course my dad's huge World War II canvas navy bag, stuffed to bursting with heavy-duty clothes. We didn't take our golden retriever, Daisy, because she disapproved of firearms. She would prance around the car with her tail wagging until she saw the long sheepskin cases containing the shotguns, then drop her head and fold her tail between her legs and slink towards the house, opting to spend a weekend on the couch instead of coming out with the boys.

With the trunk and the back seat loaded, we'd head out into the countryside, which was never so beautiful as in autumn. By nightfall, we'd be bouncing along the mud road towards Marsh Manor, our hunting lodge, a decrepit, mouse-infested old City of Winnipeg trolley bus that my dad and his buddies had mounted, on blocks, next to a prairie marsh that the government map called Lake 15.

That night, while coyotes howled in the nearby woods and a huge harvest moon rose over the hill, they'd barbecue gigantic T-bone steaks slathered with onions. After dinner they'd play a few rounds of poker and drink a whisky or two before bed. My father's friends owned hunting dogs, but the dogs had proven themselves so citified that none were worth bringing on an actual hunting trip. I was therefore the honorary dog, and I would sit in the corner like a young Lab, wagging my tail when spoken to. There was a naughty calendar on the wall, or at least what passed for a naughty picture in those days—I think it involved a leggy redhead in gumboots and a pair of long johns—and they liked teasing me about it. "Son, you stick to the redheads and the canvasbacks, and we'll take care of the redheads and the blondes."

My dad had given me a heavy, flannel-lined arctic sleeping bag for my birthday, and I loved sleeping in it, pulling it over my head so the mice wouldn't run across my face. I'd climb into bed and fall asleep while the men were still playing cards, and then suddenly the alarm clock would be hammering. It would be five in the morning, and I'd jump out of bed because it was time to go hunting. The men, who took these trips not so much for the hunting as for the food, would of course begin the day by preparing another vast meal, this time bacon and eggs, with thick slabs of fresh bakery bread propped up on a wire toasting rack above the flaming hole in the old cast-iron wood stove. When the toast was browned, my dad would slather on butter and strawberry jam and then stack the slabs in a tall column atop the stove, ready to be deployed when the tin plates were warmed and the bacon and eggs were ready. After breakfast, we dressed in several layers of heavy clothes and launched our canoes into the marsh.

As we dipped our paddles, skim ice bonked against the canvas hull of the canoe. There were millions of stars all around us. It was like canoeing through the sky, like being Winkin' Blinkin' and Nod, who paddled on a river of crystal light into a sea of dew. Invisible wings whistled past in the darkness. When we got to the grassy point where we would hunt, my dad would maneuver the canoe and I would drop the decoys in the water, making sure the anchor lines were untangled and the birds floated upright. Then we'd retire into the high cane grass along the shore and make ourselves a hiding place with a clear view of the decoys. Even on a cold morning it was cozy once you got tucked into the reeds, made yourself a padded seat with a burlap sack, and unscrewed the lid of the thermos to drink some of the steaming hot chocolate that my dad had prepared while the bacon was frying.

12

By now, the eastern sky would be streaked with pink, heating the air just enough to waken the breeze and set the cane grass swaying. Morning was coming, and with it came the exciting prospect of the appearance of the ducks. If an early mallard streaked through the sunrise, clawing overhead, my dad would stand up and point his gun. Bang! The gun would shoot flame, and even if he missed (Damn!), ducks being difficult to hit, I was pleased to watch the duck streak away and smell the delicious gunpowder on the morning air. Right now all my friends, poor saps, were trudging to school, and I felt extraordinarily lucky to be here.

During my first couple of years on the hunt, I wasn't allowed to shoot. My job was to run around in the bulrushes and look for downed birds. But finally, I got my chance. It was a beautiful sunny day, so lazy and warm that the duckies weren't flying. At eleven o'clock in the morning, my dad decided we'd give it another fifteen minutes, then head in. "Can I hold the gun?" I asked him. "And take a shot if a duck comes?"

No reasonable man would have enjoyed sharing a tippy canoe with a small boy armed with a large shotgun. But my dad liked giving people more credit than they probably deserved, and he handed me the gun. It was his Remington, a Model 870 Wingmaster. It was almost as long as I was, and I loved its impressive heft, its scarred woodwork, and its sweet aroma of gun oil. A moment later, as if dispatched by God, a flying duck appeared out of nowhere, dodging through the cattails at high speed. I snapped off the safety, placed the front sight in front of the duck and pulled the trigger. The gun slammed me in the shoulder, making an enormous boom, and the duck crashed into the water. Oh my god, I thought. I've killed one.

We paddled out into the marsh. The duck was floating on the calm blue water. There wasn't a mark on the bird, and it was stone dead. My father didn't congratulate me or tell me I'd made a nice shot. He was the sort of man who didn't talk at moments like that. But I think I caught a trace of a private smile as he picked up the duck and handed it to me. It was a beautiful little blue-winged teal, limp, warm, and radiantly feathered. I examined its lacquered bill and leathery feet, and later that day, in the front seat of the car, I held it in my hands all the way back to Winnipeg. For days, I kept the duck out in the garage and spent many hours visiting with it. The duck made a great temporary pet, albeit a dead one.

I was now washed in the blood, as they say, a certified duck hunter, and over the next few years my father taught me how to become a better one. He showed me how to set up decoys and blinds in a grain field so that waterfowl, as they circle endlessly, won't detect a trick. He taught me how to identify ducks at a distance, how to pluck them and clean them, and how to cook them for dinner. A fat mallard, stuffed with apples and roasted at 450 Fahrenheit, was in fact the first meal I ever cooked for myself.

But duck hunting wasn't simply about shooting ducks. It was about everyday life, and as always, my father wasn't inclined to make speeches about it. He tended to instruct by inference, allowing me to make my own decisions. If I screwed up, the only sign was a certain lack of feedback. By fine-tuning my powers of intuition, I began to realize that even if you're hungry, you probably shouldn't just open the fridge and stand there stuffing food in your mouth. You shouldn't offer your own fascinating opinion when other people are talking. You shouldn't claim you hit every duck that falls within eighty yards of your blind. And you shouldn't rehash a day's hunt by reminding everyone of what a good shot you were, especially if it's true.

My father and his friends came from a different generation. They didn't switch on automatic, hundred-watt smiles when posing for photographs. They didn't schmooze. And they didn't believe in lathering kids with compliments and "positive reinforcement." Today, not many kids use the prefix "Mister" when they are speaking to their father's friends. But even though I knew my father's friends very well, I would no sooner call them by their first names than I would snatch the cigar out of their mouths. Like my dad, they were lofty figures in my eyes, characters who belonged on Mount Rushmore. Because they were so reluctant to offer praise, I worked twice as hard to get it.

Eventually I grew up. I became a man myself, with a car and a girlfriend and hunting buddies of my own, and I became uninterested in hunting with Mr. Caton and Mr. Bole and all the other demigods of my dad's acquaintance. They didn't seem to take it as seriously. They'd stand there drinking coffee while ducks flew right overhead. They would miss easy shots, over and over, and then joke about it. "How was your hunting trip?" I'd ask my dad when he got home.

"The weather was beautiful," he'd answer. "On Thursday afternoon there was a stunning migration of redtail hawks. Hundreds of them."

"How many ducks did you get?"

He'd shrug. "We got enough."

Sure, Dad. I'd gotten into the habit of evaluating a duck hunt by a single measure—body count. When the old guys blundered around in the marsh and came home almost empty-handed, talking about migrating hawks and beautiful weather, I knew they were putting on a brave face. They couldn't hunt very well anymore, and they didn't want to admit it.

One day my dad went up to Netley Marsh for a hunt with a few of his cronies, and while he was there, his friend Dick Bonnycastle died of a heart attack. I had to drive up and tell

him Dick was gone. Dick was part of the original gang of
elders. He was an ally of mine. He was a good shot, and he
flew his own plane. He had also built one of the biggest publishing companies in the world, Harlequin Books. He'd died
behind the controls of his Cessna, like the grand outdoors-
man he was, and I hoped that if I ever got old, two or three
centuries from now, I would make a similarly theatrical exit.

Pretty soon the other members of his group started
appearing in the obituaries, one by one, and my dad's hunting
trips became fewer and farther between. His old Remington
pump hung untouched on its rack on the knotty pine wall
of his rec room, and when I had a good hunt, I would take
him a few mallards for his Sunday dinner. On his seventy-
fifth birthday, I decided to take him out for a special treat, a
first-class hunt. I would try to show him the sort of adventure
that he'd shown me as a kid, and thereby thank him for introducing me to waterfowl hunting. The only question was,
where would we go?

Marsh hunting was out of the question. Mud flats and
tippy boats would be too much for a man of his age. Field
shooting is always an uncertain proposition. At least half the
time, field shoots end up a bust, and I was looking for a high-
percentage opportunity. Luckily there was a slight shift in
the migratory flyway that year, and eastern Manitoba began
swarming with large flocks of geese. Forty miles east of Winnipeg an old hunting buddy of mine, Paul Craft, lives in a
gorgeous log house next to a wooded creek. Paul agreed to
do some scouting to line up a field for the three of us. A few
nights later, the phone rang.

"Okay, we're in business," Paul announced, without identi-
fying himself. "They're in the cornfield down the road."

"Canadas?"

"Both snows and Canadas, two or three thousand of them. They've been there a couple of days, and they're flying right in, acting like they own the field."

"Great. Count us in."

"Better be in the yard by six."

My dad was skeptical when I called and asked him if he wanted to go on a goose hunt the next morning. "I don't even have a hunting license."

I reminded him Canadian Tire was open until nine o'clock at night. He had plenty of time to pick up a license and some shells. "This is going to be a good shoot," I told him. "You don't want to miss this."

I could hear Dad chuckle. He'd been on plenty of wild goose chases in his day, and he had a healthy skepticism about both the predictability of the birds and the dependability of his eldest son.

The next morning I got up at four-thirty. As I loaded the Jeep in the garage behind my house, I could hear the beagle-yelp of migrating geese drifting down from skies high above the city. I drove over to my dad's, picked him up, and we headed out of town. Ah yes, the old feeling. The game was afoot. The Trans-Canada Highway was deserted, and the radio whispered with atmospheric skip, picking up wispy scraps of country music and talk shows from Kansas City or Chicago. They were the same talk shows with the same screwball callers that we had listened to on mornings like this many years ago. But now, I was driving and my dad was in the passenger seat. The tables were turned, but I could still feel the silent scrutiny of my driving ability every time I flicked on a turn signal and pulled out to pass a semi.

We arrived at Paul's forty minutes later. As we pulled into the driveway the lights were shining yellow in the kitchen and the eastern sky was turning pink. Coyotes were singing from the woods, and a group of Labrador pups rolled around on the deck. The whole scene looked like something out of an old L.L. Bean hunting calendar, except that when Paul came out he was wearing pressed slacks and a necktie. "Unexpected business complication," he said. "So I can't join you. But I set up the blind, and you guys can hunt the field on your own."

I think my father would have been just as happy to spend the morning doing odd jobs on Paul's property and horsing around with the Labrador pups. But the sky was lightening and I was keen to ambush some geese. Following Paul's truck out of the yard, we cruised along a grassy tractor trail, then out into a cornfield. Broken cornstalks rattled and thumped on the underside of the Jeep as we followed Paul to the centre of the field, where a tall, odd-looking blind stood out like a phone booth. "What's this?" my father said.

I told him that Paul and I had started using this type of blind a few years ago. We hung a roll of chicken wire with cornstalks and staked it upright in the field, and the geese didn't seem to mind it a bit. Paul wished us luck and left for his meeting. We set up thirty-six decoys in a ragged V-shape upwind of the blind. Then we got settled in the blind, along with the two wooden crates that Paul had thoughtfully left for us as seats. My father was vastly amused by all of this, and I had to remind him to load his gun. "The geese could show up any minute," I said.

He chuckled again. He had good reason to question the odds of bagging a goose. When he was young, wild geese were rare on the Prairies, and nothing was more precious for Thanksgiving dinner than a big Canada goose. In the past four decades, since wetland conservation groups like Ducks Unlimited have established waterfowl refuges all up and down the Mississippi flyway, wild goose populations have exploded. In some places, there are so many that city people regard them as a nuisance, "rats with feathers." But waterfowl hunters continue to be reverential about geese, and I couldn't imagine a better birthday present for my father.

We sat in silence for the next ten minutes, watching the daylight gradually intensify the color of the russet cornfield. Coyotes were yipping along the river, and occasionally a flock of unseen ducks whispered overhead. I decided to give my dad first crack at any geese that came in. Don't outshoot him too badly, I lectured myself. Remember, it's his birthday.

Unlike ducks, geese usually wait until broad daylight before they start moving. The sun had no sooner started to spill over the horizon than I heard a distant yelp. A ragged line of pencil checks appeared above the treeline. "Here they come!" I hissed.

The geese crossed the line of trees on the eastern side of the field, then cupped their wings and glided toward us, leveling off only at the last moment to give our decoys a dutiful fly-around. Geese are usually cautious when they approach a field, and a bit of movement or even a glint of sunlight on a plastic decoy can scare them off. But Paul was right. These geese behaved as if they owned the field. After turning onto final approach, they dropped their gear and glided into the decoys.

Despite my promise to myself, when a large goose broke ranks and came gliding right over the blind, I couldn't resist raising my gun. I swung the front bead past the bird's cheek patch and jerked the trigger. Even as the gun went off I realized, with the twinge of self-loathing so familiar to the choke artist, that I'd not only broken my vow but missed the bird.

My father's Remington was now booming beside me. I twisted the gun upward and tried a second shot, focusing on a section of open sky about a yard ahead of my fleeing goose. This might have been a decent lead under normal circumstances, but since the goose was more or less stationary, clawing for altitude overhead, the shot charge had no more effect than to change the bird's expression from amazement to disgust. With an aggressive thrash of his wings he flew away.

My dad stepped out of the blind and walked toward two large geese that were lying on the stubble, stone dead.

So much for embarrassing him with my marksmanship. A few minutes later another flock appeared, snow geese this time, and my father once again shot a double. He made it look both awkward and graceful, clambering to his feet with some difficulty, settling the gun against his shoulder and crumpling first one goose, then another. I managed to tweak a bird myself this time, a juvenile goose that suddenly lost fire in one engine and crash-landed into the stubble. As soon as I picked it up, I heard a distant yelping and had to rush back to the blind. For the next hour that's how it went, one flock after another, with my father outshooting me on every pass. Then, after a ninth dead goose had been added to the pile at our feet, he shucked an empty cartridge out of his gun and announced, "Okay, that's enough."

"What do you mean? We haven't got our limit yet."

I'd killed the last goose cleanly and was beginning to recover my groove. This was the end of a long bad-luck streak, and I wanted payback. I couldn't count the number of mornings I'd gone goose hunting and gotten skunked, lying in mud in the freezing rain while birds by the thousands settled into a field a mile away.

"We don't need a limit," he said, jacking the last shell out of his gun.

It was his birthday, so I couldn't argue the point. I didn't know it was his last hunt, but I suppose he did. Soon enough he would be crippled by a stroke, and the only geese he would see would be those flying high above the roof of his hospital. So he wanted to end his hunting career the way he had always lived it, as a man of fairness and moderation. He stepped out of the blind and walked toward a dead bird that was lying among the decoys, and then it happened.

A honk like the squeeze-horn of an old Ford Model "A" sounded in the distance and a very large, lone Canada goose came beating out of the sunrise. Standing at my dad's side, I watched the bird approach. I was pleased that I hadn't unloaded my gun. Solitary geese can be dumb at times. Although we were standing right in the open, the goose assumed the decoys were long-lost buddies and flew right toward us, honking plaintively.

"Should I shoot?"

My father didn't answer. In only a moment, the goose would cross the threshold into gun range. But time slowed down, and I became sharply aware of the importance of this instant, the layering of memory, the many watercolor paintings I'd seen depicting this exact scene—this same sunrise, these same two hunters frozen in their tracks, and the silent figure of the older one, the father, standing there like a patient instructor, watching that last goose approach and refusing to answer his son's question.

Instead of lifting the gun and shooting at the goose, I lifted my arm and waved. The old goose flared in alarm, and we both stood there and watched it fly away.

Cool
HOUND LUKE

◇◇◇◇◇

*I*t's too bad that the people who know the answers to the world's problems are all driving cabs or going to university. When I was a twenty-year-old English major I was much smarter than I am now. I was so wise that I didn't see the necessity of attending class, or of wasting time writing term papers for professors who couldn't see the obvious connection between the Holy Bible and the lyrics of the Grateful Dead.

Instead of spending my days in form-fit plastic chairs, listening to establishment blather, I preferred to spend my days at the campus pub, where the boys and I played shuffleboard, drank beer, and wrapped up social problems that had baffled economists for centuries. One of the most troubling issues we tackled was the fact that so-called modern science had yet to produce the perfect hunting dog.

This was important because in the autumn, when we weren't holding court in the campus pub, we were skipping classes to go bird hunting. From Labor Day to November, there were always boots, shells, and a Remington pump gun in the trunk of my car. Okay, technically it was my dad's car. But he was the one who'd gotten me hooked on hunting, so he had to share a good portion of the blame for my irresponsibility. That's how I looked at it.

On weekends, we would normally go to a party on Friday night, stay out until three or four o'clock in the morning, and then head out of the city, speeding across a hundred miles of godforsaken prairie toward the pothole country of Neepawa or the marshes of Glenboro. The lonesome tunes on the radio, the hypnotic rhythm of the broken yellow line, and the raspy snores of the boys in the back seat sometimes cast a spell on our designated driver, and I remember more than one occasion when we sailed off the end of a T-bone intersection and landed nose-first in a muddy field. One night we had to sleep on the concrete floor of a service station. Another night we ran out of gas, and I had to siphon a few gallons from a passing Mountie's car. The officer didn't mind giving us the gas, but I do recall his look of disgust as I lay on the road with a rubber hose in my hand, fuel spewing on my face.

Most of the time, we made it to our intended hunting area. Having been up all night, we used coffee, cigarettes, and an occasional Jimi Hendrix song, played at high volume on the car radio, to keep our wits sharp. Drowsiness, our foe, kept circling around and leaping on us from behind. By midmorning, sometimes a task as elementary as fetching the car and driving down a simple tractor path to pick up the boys at the other end of the field required so much concentration that you had to talk to yourself in a loud voice just to stay awake. By noon, we would be scattered throughout the marsh, lying face down on some brambled mudbank with drool leaking

23

from our lips and spiders crawling on our eyelids. The night before, though, when the party was still thumping in our nerves and the long dark highway was calling, staying up and going hunting seemed like a brilliant idea.

Our heartland was the Manitoba prairie. From the air it looks like tartan, a bolt of cloth stretched flat across the province. The prairie is a patchwork of farms and granaries, mile roads that chop up the landscape like the lines on graph paper. Modern agriculture, the most destructive industry of the last century, has long ago succeeded in converting most of the Great Plains into a science project. But several of the thousand-odd species that once inhabited the prairie still make an okay sort of living there, and it was our desire to kill them. We didn't put much thought into the logical inconsistency between our high-minded condemnation of big business, factory farming, and the Vietnam war and our own eagerness to shoot the survivors on sight. But if pressed, we might have held our palms over our hearts and quoted Sitting Bull, who, for some reason, many young men of my generation had adopted as a role model. (Bury Our Hearts at Wounded Knee!) A poster-sized daguerreotype of the great Lakota warrior was tacked to the wall above my bed, and he offered his own explanation. "We will always be hunters," he said. "And when the buffalo are gone we will hunt mice."

We often cut classes and took afternoon trips to the grain fields outside the city. It wasn't exactly like crossing the Manitoba prairie of the 1800s, when the flower-spattered expanse of bluestem rippled like a green Atlantic in the wind and, according to one account, passing waterfowl were so legion that "it was impossible for us to converse above the din." But the prairie still supported enough ducks and geese to provide us with a bit of occasional shooting. When we couldn't find any ducks and geese, we shot tin cans. Most of us owned hunting dogs, or at least our fathers did. The dogs had registration papers, serial numbers tattooed under their ears, and they all looked like refined examples of the dog breeder's art. But when it came to actually hunting, they were useless.

My friend Kerry had a Hungarian Vizla named Hogan. The Vizla breed is alleged to be an effective hunter of all species of upland game, and Hogan seemed motivated enough. He was so keen, in fact, that as soon as we left the city he would start moaning. For hours, as Kerry drove his dad's station wagon around the countryside, Hogan would cry, yip, and slobber like a hyena. When the noise became unbearable we'd let him out of the car, and he would take off at a flat run, chasing blackbirds, gophers, dairy cows, and anything else that wasn't a fence post.

Many generations of careful breeding have apparently given the Vizla a nonexistent undercoat. Whenever it began to rain or, worse yet, sleet, Hogan would begin shuddering like a skid row wino. One day we succeeded in winging a mallard that had glided down into a little oxbow swamp along the river. It was a hot day, for late September, and since Hogan was supposed to be a hunting dog, we asked him to retrieve the bird. It didn't exactly cost him his life, but for a while it seemed he was going to be the first hunting dog in history to die of hypothermia while simultaneously suffering from sunstroke.

Buckshot was a German shorthaired pointer. My brother-in-law Bill chose that breed because they're supposed to be strong, versatile hunting dogs, well suited for both waterfowl and upland game. Buckshot had a huge head, as big as the butt end of a tree, but it didn't seem to have a brain inside it. When he was in the mood for a nap, he would spin in a slow circle for up to a full minute, muttering to himself, before

25

finally flopping down on the carpet. But he was more durable than Hogan, and he could run into a barbed wire fence and cut long gouges in his face without seeming to care. Bill spent a lot of time teaching him whistle commands, hand signals, and voice commands like "go back." I never fully understood what "go back" was supposed to mean, and apparently neither did Buckshot, because I can still hear Bill hollering across the marsh, again and again, as his well-intentioned but completely dimwitted dog galloped around in the cattails, trying to figure out how to "go back."

Buckshot's worst habit was "breaking to gunfire," that is, taking off in search of downed birds whenever someone fired a gun. We tried everything to cure him of this annoying habit. Bill finally seized upon the idea of holding Buckshot's leash in order to deliver a darn good yank when he bolted. I volunteered to hold him, wrapping the line around my waist a few times. It never occurred to me that it might not be smart to be standing there with a rope around my waist when a ninety-pound dog hit the end of it going full speed. But after I flew through the air and did a face plant in the mud, we reassessed the strategy and decided it might work better if we tied the leash to the bumper of Bill's car, a Volkswagen Beetle. Bill fired the gun. When Buck hit the end of the rope, the bumper separated from the car with a loud bang and went bouncing down the road after him.

We always had dogs in our family, but none of them were any good at bird hunting. Toby slept all day. Billy was a hoodlum who liked chasing cats. Daisy, our golden retriever, had been bred for the field, and when she was a puppy she seemed like the perfect duck dog. She was eager to please and did very well on the hunting dog IQ test, a quiz you can conduct at home by putting a dog biscuit on the floor and laying a towel

26

on top of it. (That new tea towel of your mother's should do nicely.) Check your watch and see how long it takes for the dog to figure out that she must somehow remove the towel, rather than claw or chew her way through it. A smart dog takes about forty-five seconds to sort it out. Daisy took only fifteen.

Daisy had a good thick coat, and she liked a long swim on a cold October day. She even liked a bit of barroom singing now and then. If you came home late at night, feeling benevolent, you could sing her a few rich verses of "Daisy, Daisy, Give Me Your Answer Do." She would express her appreciation by retrieving a sheepskin bedroom shoe, jamming her forehead into your lap, and thumping the couch with her tail.

Daisy's only flaw was that she was "gun shy," a condition usually blamed on the dog's owner. Dog experts talk about the intelligence and personality of individual dogs, but if a dog displays a quirk of individuality, faulty training is invariably cited as the cause. "Well you see, you frightened her with a loud noise when she was young." To train dogs to tolerate gunfire, you're supposed to expose them to guns when they're puppies, shooting a cap pistol at mealtime, then graduating to louder shots (presumably shooting off the 12-gauge shotguns and other heavy ordnance outside). But Daisy had never had a bad experience with loud noises, so it must have been her choice. She was, in some ways, more evolved than some of the male human beings she shared the house with.

In our house, firearms were as common as hockey sticks, and you didn't have to go farther than the wall above the fireplace to find one. But this casual treatment of guns had ended when Daisy joined the family. Like our own namby-pamby anti-gun activist, she refused to go into any room where firearms were displayed. My dad tried to take her hunting a few times, but as soon as he unsheathed his shotgun

27

Daisy would hit the trail, tuck her tail down and run off down the road without looking back. That was saying a lot, because she worshipped my father, followed him everywhere, and in the evening, while he read the newspaper, ordinarily sat by his side with her head on his knee. My dad forgave Daisy and I think quietly loved her for her Quaker tendencies. But my brother and I would sometimes tease her by raising a baguette to our shoulders, pointing it at the ceiling light, and making ray-gun noises ("yibble yibble") just to watch her shudder with disgust and crawl under the table.

The only truly great hunting dog I ever knew was a shaggy mongrel named Luke. I made his acquaintance in my early twenties, when I had decided that I wanted to become a writer. I quit university, bought a canoe and some camping equipment, and set off into the backwoods to find a life of rustic simplicity. My only role models were literary figures like Hemingway's Nick Adams and Thoreau, and I'm sure that if Walden Pond or the Big Two-Hearted River had been within striking distance of my home I would have naively headed off in one of those directions, imagining that I could pick up where those other guys had left off. Going to the family cottage seemed unambitious, so I drove east into northern Ontario until I hit a little town called Minaki. Pitching my tent, I got a job working as a fishing guide and did some writing in the evening. I thought I was just going to stay for the summer. But I met some friends, eventually built a houseboat, and ended up staying for seven years. One of my friends in Minaki was Luke.

Luke was a lumbering character whom everyone regarded as a member of the community. Luke lived with Buck and Lori and then he lived with Dave, but he got along with everyone. He enjoyed rambling around the woods with his girlfriend, a pretty husky named Abby, and he made a casual point of dropping in on his various human friends around dinnertime, where he was usually offered some table scraps and an open space on the floor.

Luke was a mix of collie and St. Bernard, and in his prime he weighed over a hundred pounds. He had big, dark, intelligent eyes that would narrow with understanding when you talked to him. His collie ancestry had given him the herding instinct, and when small children were around, Luke acted like he was on duty. He'd lie among them, keep an eye on things, and suffer their ear-pulls and choke-holds with avuncular calm. But Luke was no teddy bear. His St. Bernard bloodline made him fiercely protective, and his fights with other dogs were terrifying bloodbaths. He lorded over a vast, undefined no-trespass zone that other large carnivores entered at their peril. I once saw him sprint across the yard and throw his shoulder into a three-hundred-pound male black bear, which somersaulted to its feet, took a roundhouse swing at Luke, and then scrambled up a tree, unwilling to mix it up with a dog who had so clearly lost his mind.

In the fall, Luke loved going hunting with his human pals. If a group of guys were going down the lake to look for deer, he would stand on the bow of the boat with his ears flapping in the wind, impervious to the bitter cold, eager to pursue the quest and help out in whatever way he could. He wasn't so much an animal as one of the boys in a fur coat. His head swiveled constantly as he checked out the shoreline, and more than once he spotted deer before anyone else did. When he saw wildlife, Luke would stiffen from head to tail and give you a dire look, indicating by his glances and body language the direction of the animal.

On autumn afternoons, I often went for a walk in the woods to see if I could hunt up a grouse for dinner. Luke

29

enjoyed these excursions, and I liked taking him along, not
just because he was an asset to the hunt but because he was
my buddy. As we walked through the bush, Luke would pad
alongside me until we eventually heard the scuttle of dead
leaves and the telltale peep-peep of a nearby ruffed grouse.
Then Luke would slink over and we would have a conference.
"Okay, Luke," I'd whisper. "I think there's a partridge inside
that clump of willows. I want you to go around the far side
and flush him out toward me."

If Luke didn't understand completely, he'd stop, fifty steps
away, and look back for hand signals. Once he knew the game
plan, he'd pad into the bush and the grouse would flush away
from him, right toward me if it worked out right. Luke had
an uncanny instinct for knowing when a hunt was afoot, and
he hated being left behind. One time he'd gotten sprayed
by a skunk, and I didn't want to take him along because he
smelled so bad. I was loading the van to go hunting when I
saw him coming. I slipped into the van and crouched there,
perfectly quiet, and watched him through the curtains. Fifty
yards away, he stopped, lowered his nose to the ground, and
then took up my trail. When he reached the van he threw his
big feet against the window and peered in at me, wearing an
expression that said, Oh, no, you don't.

St. Bernards don't usually live for more than nine or ten
years. But Luke's collie genes served him well, and he was
still going strong at twelve years old. When rheumatism and
failing eyesight made it impossible for him to continue his
hobo ways, it seemed as if his days were numbered. There's
no place in a backwoods town for a dog that can't defend
himself, and I think Luke would have been fatally injured by
one of his rivals if he'd stayed in Minaki. Luckily for him, I
was moving. I'd written a couple of novels by then, the last of

which had actually found a publisher, and I was ready to try to make a living as a writer in the city. I couldn't stay here, anyway. Life in the backwoods is a never-ending scramble. You throw most of your resources into just staying alive, fixing things, hauling water, cutting firewood. In the wintertime, you spend hours every day tending the wood burner. In the city, you adjust the thermostat and go back to your writing. The day I was packing to go, Luke sat nearby, watching. He had been on the losing end of a recent dustup, and there was a lumpy slash across the top of his forehead. It was a dark autumn afternoon, and the wind smelled of snow. As I loaded the van, Luke wore the same look of disbelief he'd worn when I was trying to sneak off on a hunting trip without him. He didn't seem to have much of a future here. So I made a few calls, and when I headed for the city, he was sleeping in the van behind me.

I rented a basement apartment in the city, and Luke moved in with me. It wasn't a very good arrangement for a dog who'd lived in the woods all his life, and Luke had a hard time adjusting. He didn't understand why so many other dogs presumed to live in his neighborhood, and when we walked to the store he growled at the interlopers. He didn't like men in uniform, whether postal workers or cops, and when anyone knocked at the door of the apartment he leaped up and roared, assuming it was a bear trying to break in. One night my friend Paul Sweatman showed up at the door. When he shook my hand and slapped me on the back, Luke flew into action. He knocked Paul down, pressed two big front paws against his chest, and growled softly, warning Paul that if he hit me again he was dead. I would always yell at Luke when he overreacted, but he would just give me a look that said, Sorry, but that's who I am.

We tried to make a go of it. I took Luke out to the Assiniboine Forest periodically so that he could go for a run, and when I had an errand downtown I would take him along. If I was going into an office building or restaurant, I'd explain the situation to him. ("I'm going to a meeting and I'll be back in an hour. Wait right here and don't talk to anybody, okay?") I would never tie him up, because he'd never worn a rope and it was too late to start now. He would more or less nod, then wait for an hour or more on the sidewalk outside, sitting like a great stuffed exhibit, ignoring all the pedestrians going past.

It wasn't a good situation, for Luke or for me, and eventually my older sister Wendy volunteered to take him. Wendy lived in a big house with a big yard, and she rode horses almost every day, which gave Luke a chance to run in the woods. When they came home from riding she would feed him a big platter of roast beef with gravy, and then he would sleep on a flannel mattress in front of the fireplace. His front leg was crooked from an ancient contest with a bear. His face was crisscrossed with the scars of a hundred brawls, including one in which an otter lured him into the water and tried to drown him. But he was happy with my sister, who doted on him and called him "the best thing that ever happened to me." Fate doesn't usually offer up happy endings for old campaigners like Luke. But sometimes it does.

One day, duck hunting south of the city, I winged a mallard that fluttered down into some tall grass by a marsh. I searched for a long time but couldn't find the duck. Driving all the way back to the city, I pulled into my sister's driveway. Luke was sleeping in the sun on the back deck. "Luke," I said, "we're bringing you out of retirement." He rose stiffly to his feet and climbed into the van.

An hour later, we arrived back at the scene. There was a warm south wind blowing, and the cane grass was rippling in

32

the wind. I waved toward the slough. "Hunt him up, Luke." He lifted his head and sniffed the breeze. I watched him move slowly into the tall grass, quartering back and forth like a hammerhead on a faint blood trail. Five minutes later, he limped out carrying the dead duck.

Luke took another trip a few months later. This time it was a one-way trip, to the veterinary hospital. The day after it happened, I dropped by my sister's house. Luke had been her constant companion, and she was red-eyed from crying.

I drank a cup of tea with Wendy, listening to her tearful tale of Luke's last meal. It was a dark November afternoon, and when I left her house it was snowing. Walking out to my van, I spotted one of Luke's wolf-like paw prints. It was the only physical thing he'd left the world, and by morning it would be gone.

Footprints

IN THE SAND

◇◇◇◇◇

*T*here are no signs marking the hilltop in life. And until you spot the subtle changes in terrain, you might not even notice that you're heading down the other side.

Middle age doesn't necessarily mean that your health is failing. Or that finally, a cashier in a restaurant asks you if you qualify for the senior's discount. It just means that you can't do certain things anymore. You can't spend your afternoons sitting on the dock of the bay. You can't drive to the coast with a dog named Boo. You can't do it because you don't have the damned time. Some guys cope with this realization by stepping up the pace, by working harder to earn their first million dollars. Other guys embark on physical fitness regimes, or become obsessed with younger women. I got serious about fishing.

Fishing is basically an amusement. But when I hit middle age I began to take it more seriously, accepting it as a paral-

lel career that required work and investment. I began buy-
ing better-quality tackle and taking better care of it. I began
working my way through the required authors. My gaze began
wandering past my favorite lake to far-flung exotic locations.
On snowy nights when the wind pawed at the door, I'd sit by
the fireplace and flip through the classic textbooks.

The color plates were like windows to another world. One
photo showed the legendary A.J. McLane standing in a New
Zealand stream with a big brown trout. Another photo showed
his wife, a blonde beauty, holding a big roosterfish she caught
on the coast of Mexico in '59. Other books and other photos
showed Scottish castles, Alaskan halibut, and the huge blue
marlin that Ernest Hemingway caught in the Gulf Stream off
the Bahamian island of Bimini. As I read the books, I could
hear a clock ticking in the background. You only live once.
It was clear that if I was going to experience some of these
places, I'd better get started.

My friend Paul Quarrington, like me, was itching to
explore some exotic fishing spots. In talking about our favorite writers one day, I discovered P.Q. was likewise a fan of
Hemingway's novels. We decided we would go down to
Bimini, where Hemingway lived for a while, and see if the
place lived up to his writing. A few months later, we boarded
a Grumman flying boat at Chalk's Air Service in Miami and
headed east across the Florida Strait, bound for the islands.

An ungainly old crate with thunderous engines, the Grumman is precisely the sort of airplane you need for taking a
journey into the past. The ride was bumpy but the scenery
was stunning, with thunderheads all around us and sunlight
glittering on the wrinkled ocean far below. From this height
the edge of the Gulf Stream was a sudden line of dark blue,
almost purple water. Forty-five miles wide, the Stream flows

north at three miles per hour past Florida, the Carolinas, Virginia, and New England, then caroms off the Grand Banks and pushes eastward, conveying heated subtropical water toward Britain and Europe. It's like an oceanic beltway, rotating clockwise past the coasts of Spain and Africa and then returning in a westerly direction toward the Caribbean. On this leg of its journey, the Gulf Stream is highly saline and rich with plankton. As it passes the Bahamas it supports such a variety of fish that big-game anglers have long regarded it as a sort of marine equivalent of the Serengeti.

Half an hour after taking off, we raised Bimini on the horizon. The pilot cut the engines, glided down and made a graceful belly-flop onto the jade-green waters of the lagoon. It's a strange sensation, sitting in a flying boat, because as you look out the portholes you realize you're actually sitting below the level of the water. With the engines sputtering, we taxied to shore, where the pilot gunned the throttles and we improbably drove up onto dry land. This is the same type of airplane in which the three boys in the movie version of *Islands in the Stream* arrive to visit with their dad, played by George C. Scott, who is playing the role of Thomas Hudson, who in turn is playing the role of Hemingway.

Paul and I went into the customs shack and presented our luggage to a uniformed young Bahamian, who scowled at us and prodded our bags with the disdain common to every customs officer on the planet. Hauling our luggage outside, we stood on the main road and flagged down one of the island's rare taxi cabs. There are only a few roads on Bimini, so most islanders rely on golf carts, which are fast enough to flatten you if you forget they're whispery silent and will come up behind you on the left side of the road.

Our hotel was the Bimini Blue Water Inn, a disheveled string of buildings on a sandy ridge overlooking the ocean.

36

The yard was piled with cinder blocks and discarded, rust-covered propane tanks. Our cabin was so narrow that you had to turn sideways to squeeze past the beds. Across the road, down a crooked set of concrete stairs, was a white-sand beach without a soul on it. We were tired from our long trip, and we looked forward to changing into our trunks and going for a long swim.

When Hemingway came here in 1935, he wasn't quite famous yet. True, he had four reasonably successful books under his belt, and a string of outdoorsy articles in some of America's larger magazines. But the big prizes, the Nobel and the Pulitzer, were still to come, and he was broke. Two ex-wives, three sons, and a freewheeling lifestyle had drained his moderate resources. A more cautious individual might have decided that it was time to settle down and maybe get a teaching post or some kind of steady job. But Hemingway didn't care about money; he cared about life. Bluffing the editor of *Esquire,* he got an advance on articles he hadn't written yet, purchased a custom-built thirty-eight-foot wooden launch he named *Pilar,* gathered his three sons, and headed for the open sea.

On June 7, 1935, Hemingway and his boys landed on North Bimini. He rented a house on the beach and wrote about it in a letter to his friend Sara Murphy: "It's a lovely old white, clapboard, three-bedroom house on a seven mile long surf bathing clear sand beach. No insects there and the water is absolutely clear Gulf Stream and is always clear but never cold. The house is on a ridge that overlooks the ocean and the lagoon and is only $20.00 a month! It blows a big breeze every day and the boys swim all morning and fish all afternoon. They are crazy about it and I don't know where in the world we could get such a beach or such water."

Paul and I went for a swim ourselves, enjoying the soothing pulse of the warm sea water on our travel-stiffened bodies,

37

then got dressed and decided to go for a walk in the evening air to see if we could find Hemingway's house. We walked for a couple of miles down the rutted Queen's Highway, but saw nothing resembling the grand house described in *Islands in the Stream*. I'd imagined that Bimini would be more like the pure, wind-swept little island in the novel. But the yards alongside the road were littered with empty liquor bottles, scraps of frayed rope, abandoned outboard motors: the usual detritus of civilization.

During the night, thunderclaps shook our little cottage, and in the morning a tropical downpour was drumming on the roof. We'd intended to go fishing. But the weather didn't look very promising, so we ate a leisurely breakfast at the neighborhood restaurant and surveyed the stormy ocean. At one point we spotted a manta ray the size of a tarpaulin gliding along the beach. "Hey, look," Paul said. "That's right where we went swimming yesterday."

"You should have been here a few days ago," the waitress said. "A twelve-foot hammerhead was swimming down that same beach."

We drank more coffee and listened to more stories from the locals. Most of them claimed to remember Hemingway, even though there wasn't a soul in the place over the age of forty.

By noon it was raining harder and showed no sign of letting up. We walked down to the wharf, where we struck up a conversation with Captain Baldwin Hinzey, a native Bahamian. He owned a twenty-eight-foot Bertram called the *Nina*. "Don't worry about this," he said. "It's going to stop raining in a few hours. Then it will be nice and calm out there, I guarantee it." He told us he charged $650 for a day of fishing, a price that churned the eggs in our stomachs. But we'd come here to catch ourselves a marlin, dammit, so we dug out our wallets and gave him the money.

Captain Baldwin would make a lousy weatherman. Half an hour later we were heading out to sea, with rain lashing the windows and heavy rollers exploding against the prow. P.Q. and I hadn't packed bad-weather gear, so we wrestled ourselves into the moldy rain pants and jackets Captain Baldwin supplied while the boat slammed its way out toward the Gulf Stream. Like a lot of charter captains, Baldwin seemed to have a streak of Captain Ahab in him. As we pounded through the driving rain he insanely barked orders at Lancer, his first mate, who was scrambling around the boat trying to get the fishing gear ready. "Lancer!" he screamed. "Get your black ass up in that tuna tower!"

The tuna tower is a sort of crow's nest up above the wheelhouse, from which the mate can get a bird's eye view of any distant signs of swarming birds and feeding fish. I doubted there would be many birds flying around in this monsoon. And with all this lightning activity, I wouldn't be standing up in a high metal tower no matter how much I was getting paid. But Lancer climbed the tower, and every once in a while Captain Baldwin would open the hatch and angrily shout up into the driving rain to determine if he had spotted any birds yet. Lancer, with eyes scrunched up in the wind and face contorted with a juvenile grin, kept shaking his head, lifting his hands in apology. With a grimace of disgust, Captain Baldwin slammed the hatch and confided that Lancer was "a pick-up mate" whom he'd grabbed off the dock at the last minute. I thought Lancer was doing a pretty good job, especially since he later admitted to us that he'd been out partying until four in the morning.

After we'd cruised for an hour, Baldwin, whom Paul and I had dubbed Captain Baldy, baited our rods with blue runners, which are smallish members of the tuna family. As he set the rods firmly in their holders he declared, "This is a good

39

spot." We seemed to be in the middle of the ocean. Paul and I glanced topside at Lancer. He looked soaked and desperate, and his dreadlocks flipped in the wind like frayed rope. As Baldy went back to the helm, Lancer started creeping down the ladder, ostensibly to help out with the chores, but Baldy screamed at him to get his ass back up in the tower.

After Paul and I flipped a coin for first turn at the rods, Baldy briefed us on the correct procedure for striking a fish. I won the toss—or lost it, given the conditions—so I climbed into the so-called fighting chair and got a good grip on the rod, which was as thick as a broomstick. Thunder was crashing overhead and rain was driving into my eyes. I cinched down the drawstring on my hood. I'd heard stories about people being pulled overboard by big marlin, so I tightened my seat belt and braced my feet against the foot rest. I remembered reading about one guy who was not only pulled overboard but was thirty feet underwater before it occurred to him to let go of the rod. Watching me from the shelter of the cabin, P.Q. puffed on a wet cigar and sent me a cheery thumbs-up. If this was the *Pilar*, he would have been making some stiff drinks and trying to get the baseball scores on the radio.

In 1935, Hemingway and his buddy Henry Strater fished these waters and hooked a thousand-pound bluefin tuna that fought for nine hours and fifty minutes. Hemingway described it in a letter to another friend: "Just when we had him whipped and on the surface showing terribly big in the searchlight at nine o'clock at night 17 miles from where he was hooked the sharks hit him. Five hit him at once. I shot three but they cut him up like a log in a planing mill. The head alone weighed 249 pounds."

I was imagining what a half-ton tuna would look like when the rod jerked in my hands. Baldwin yelled that I had a fish. P.Q. came out of the cabin and slapped me on the back. I furiously cranked the handle, but the gears inside the reel seemed to be corroded, and the handle balked and squealed as I cranked it. Somehow I managed to lift the fish to the surface. "Nice mackerel!" shouted Captain Baldy. It was indeed a nice mackerel and a true mackerel, but it was a small mackerel, maybe three pounds soaking wet. I reeled it closer to the boat. Then a shark appeared out of nowhere and chomped on my tragic fish. The shark was larger than the mackerel, but not by much.

I played tug of war with the shark for a moment and felt a sudden release of tension. When I reeled in the line there was nothing on the hook but the mackerel's head.

"You didn't reel fast enough!" Captain Baldy scolded me, unhooking the ravaged mackerel head and tossing it overboard. The head hit the water and disappeared in a swirl. If I'd been Hemingway, I would have grabbed a gun and shot the shark full of holes. Hemingway carried a Thompson submachine gun in the *Pilar,* the same model of "chopper" that Eliot Ness and his Untouchables used in their skirmishes with the Chicago mob, and he relished any opportunity to use it. "Shot 27 sharks in two weeks," he wrote. "All over ten feet long. As soon as they put their heads out we give them a burst."

Hemingway also managed to shoot himself with it. The bullets passed through his calves without striking bone, so he wasn't seriously injured. He was famously accident prone and could barely open a window without dropping it on his hand. Literary scholars have written countless essays speculating that he was tortured by self-loathing, repressed homosexuality, and so on. But one shouldn't discount the theory that much of the time he was just plain bombed.

Now it was Paul's turn in the fighting chair. After a few minutes, he hooked a skinny barracuda, which he waterskied to the boat so the sharks wouldn't eat it. Then I lost a nice grouper. (Paul and I had a slight debate over whether I could reasonably describe this grouper as "lost." As Izaak Walton once said, "No man can lose what he never had.") Then a shark gobbled one of Paul's mackerels. It looked like it had been sliced in half by a chain saw. "He cut it up like a log in a planing mill," Paul muttered. Baldy threw the mutilated mackerel over the side, where it was dive-bombed by a flock of seabirds. We were supposed to be following them, but they were following us. After they gobbled the remains of the mackerel, they lifted off the water and returned to their station about twenty feet off the stern, swerving and wafting in the wind like tiny kites. These weren't herring gulls, but tiny white terns, with scissor tails and delicate wings. When Hemingway was out here, eating raw onion sandwiches and waiting for a bite, he would occasionally pass the time trying to shoot their heads off with his .25-caliber pocket pistol.

That night P.Q. and I went for a few drinks at a local bar called the Compleat Angler. It's built of heavy timbers salvaged from an old rum runner that broke up on a nearby reef in the 1920s. The wall of the bar is covered with old photographs of Hemingway and his contemporaries with their huge fishes. We asked the bartender, a tall handsome black man, how we might go about catching a few whoppers of the type depicted. "They all be gone, man. Those boys caught 'em all!"

Since Hemingway and his cronies just threw away those big marlins, you'd think they could have left a few for the next generation. But Paul and I decided that cruising around in a big boat wasn't really our style anyway. It seemed to require more brute strength than finesse, and even if we caught a marlin, what would we do with it? Hang it on a pole and take photographs? And even if we'd wanted to go out with Captain Baldy again, we couldn't afford it. Deep-sea fishing is better suited to the sort of men Hunter S. Thompson once described as having "thick necks, small brains and fat wallets."

As we sat there drinking, Hemingway and his steely-eyed pals posing heroically all around us, we hatched a plan. Instead of going after the largest fish in the sea, we'd go after the smallest. We'd both heard stories about a legendary critter called the bonefish. The bonefish is a runt—only a couple of pounds in weight—and it's never going to win a beauty contest. With its bulbous nose, undershot mouth, and stunned expression it looks like the piscine equivalent of Woody Allen. But it's revered for its sporty qualities.

The next day we walked down to the island's sole tackle shop and inquired as to where we might find some bonefish. The guy told us that there were lots of "bones" in the area, and said our best bet was to hire an old-timer named Ansil Saunders, who was not only the best bonefishing guide in the entire Bahamas but also happened to be his uncle. He phoned Ansil for us and set up an outing for the next day. Encouraged by this turn of events, we bought some bonefish magazines, which laid out the basic strategy for catching the little mutts.

The main quality of bonefish is their extreme wariness. A badly aimed cast will send a whole school dashing away in panic. They are well camouflaged, and so difficult to see that even anglers with polarized glasses and considerable experience have a hard time locating them. Once spotted, a school of bonefish must be stalked like deer. Their feeding path must be estimated. If wading conditions are favorable, the angler might slip out of the boat and try to approach the fish on foot. If he follows the guide's whispered instructions, casts well, and twitches the lure just delicately enough to attract a feeding bonefish, the payoff is in the fish's tentative bite, then its sudden, electrifying run.

43

The next day we rose early and went to meet Ansil Saunders. He was late, on purpose, to demonstrate how lucky we were to be fishing with him. When he finally showed up in his handsome wooden boat, he scowled at us like a crusty Supreme Court justice turned law professor with no patience for another crop of bumbling freshmen. "Don't do it that way," he grumbled, as we tried climbing down the ladder to his boat. "Always climb down a ladder backwards. Don't you know that? Give me the camera bag. What kind of camera is that anyway? You need a better camera than that."

We sat down and got settled. ("Don't scrape that wood with your sandy shoes!") Ansil hit the gas, and we went speeding across the dappled green water of the shallow lagoon. On the far side we entered a mangrove swamp, still at full speed, and for the next mile we sped along through an overgrown tunnel of mangrove foliage. Eventually we emerged onto a vast tidal flat. Ansil shut off the motor, picked up his pole, and propelled us gently forward.

"You ever fish for bonefish?" he asked.

"No sir."

"You know how to use a fly rod?"

"Not really. But we'd sure like to learn."

He sniffed, shaking his head. I wondered if his grumpiness was a general all-purpose grumpiness or a deliberate grumpiness to show us he was the boss. I remembered using similar tactics when I was a young fishing guide in Minaki. My guests were wealthy businessmen, accustomed to receiving suction treatment from service personnel and underlings. The moment they stepped into your boat, it was important to establish that you were the skipper. All it took was a direct look, a firm handshake, and a few instructions about boating safety to get the point across. Ansil made the same point by

44

mostly ignoring us, staring at the water as he poled along, and telling us periodically not to shuffle our dirty feet on the varnished floor boards.

Ansil's white golf shirt had a stenciled message above the breast pocket—*Ansil Saunders, Bonefish Legend, World Record, 16 lbs*. I asked him if he'd caught a world-record bonefish. He affirmed that he had, clearly annoyed that I hadn't heard about it. We kept asking him questions, and finally he told us that he was sixty-eight years old and that his family had lived on Bimini for six generations. He learned about tides, fishing tackle, weather, and sea life from his father. He started guiding when he was sixteen and had built this boat himself. It had oak ribs, gleaming mahogany floorboards, and transom braces hand-carved from a tough local wood he called "horseflesh."

"It grows on the beach," he said. "I cut the brace from the part of the tree that faces into the wind. That's the strongest wood in the world."

"Have you ever had any famous guests?" I asked.

"I don't believe in fame," he answered. "You think fame is important?"

"I guess not."

He poled along silently, annoyed by our stupid questions. Finally he admitted that he knew Margaret Thatcher. At a party in Nassau, she had spotted him from across the room, then made her way over and introduced herself. "Who are you?" she asked.

He told her he was Ansil Saunders, Bonefish Legend.

She said she admired the strength in his face.

"I told her about horseflesh wood," he said. "I told her that Bahamian people are strong because all our lives we face hurricanes."

"What else did she say?" Paul asked.

"She said, 'The water is so beautiful here, but you know what? I can't go swimming.' I asked her why, and she said, 'Because the press would take a picture of me and then write a story about the lazy prime minister relaxing on the beach while back home everyone is out of work. When you're a politician they never leave you alone. They never miss an opportunity to make you look bad.'"

After so much rain, it was nice to feel the heat on our arms. We drifted across the flats, searching for a flash of silver or the puff of silt that could mark the path of a cruising bonefish. The white-sand bottom was patchy with turtle grass. The sky was huge, packed with high clouds, and it was so quiet that we automatically began to whisper. A shark swam past, then a stingray. Then Ansil pointed ahead. "Bonefish," he said quietly. "Over there."

P.Q. and I scrutinized the surface of the water. Ansil baited a couple of spinning rods with fresh shrimp and handed them to us. We cast in the direction of his pointed finger, and the water erupted with panicked bonefish. "You ruined it," he said. "You cast like a couple of elephants."

For the next forty minutes we made repeated attempts at fish, terrifying half a dozen schools of bonefish with our errant casting. Then our casting settled down and we began hitting them. I caught and released a nice five-pounder. A few minutes later Paul released one the same size. There were so many schools coming in with the tide that we slipped out of the boat and began wading across the flats.

I selected a spot at random and just stood there, wondering if a school would happen along. Sure enough, a quartet of large bonefish came grubbing along the bottom, heading my way. I placed a perfect cast, close enough for them to see

46

it and far enough that they weren't frightened by the splash. One of the quartet rushed to investigate, and an instant later the rod surged. The fight lasted ten minutes, resulting in a handsome six-pounder. P.Q. took a photograph and then I released the fish.

This was much superior to trolling around in a big smelly boat. We were always doing something: walking, casting, scanning the water for movement. Because our senses were keyed up, we were more alert to the translucent water, the gliding birds. When the tide began to recede, the bonefish disappeared. We climbed back into the skiff, exhausted by the tension and elated by our minor success.

Ansil opened the cooler, handing each of us a corned beef sandwich and a cold Coke. We asked him about Hemingway. He said he remembered him, although he'd been a boy at the time. "He used to walk down the street with a bottle of liquor sticking out of his back pocket. He was a big man and he thought he owned the island. My mother used to say, 'Stay away from that man. He is nothing but trouble.'"

I had no doubt Ansil was telling the truth. White Americans were the dominant class on Bimini, and in his letters Hemingway ordinarily referred to the Bahamians as "jigs." Describing evenings of revelry in the Compleat Angler, he wrote, "When anybody is tight here or feels dangerous they ask me to fight. It's a local pastime called 'Trying him.' Have fought four times in the last two weeks—twice with bare fists, twice with gloves. All knockouts. Knocked out the biggest and toughest jig on island in less than a minute."

We ate our sandwiches as Ansil poled the boat along. Groups of smallish barracuda held crossways in the channel beneath us, darting away from the shadow of the boat, then gliding back to their holding position. We also saw sharks,

47

lots of them. Most of them were lemon sharks—three to four feet in length, thirty to forty pounds in weight. They made a tempting sight as they cruised past with their dorsal fins out of the water, and when one came within range I tried to interest it with a shrimp, casting the bait out in front of it. The shark turned toward the shrimp, then shied away when it saw me. I made ready to cast again but Ansil cautioned me about fooling around with sharks, even the small ones. "If you hurt a shark, he'll hurt you back. One time I was with these boys and we spotted a huge tiger shark in shallow water. They wanted to kill it, but every time they threw a harpoon at it, the shark charged over and bit the boat. When sharks get angry, their skin tightens up and the harpoon won't penetrate. So they kept throwing the harpoon, and it kept attacking the boat. Finally it grabbed the motor and started pulling the transom off, so those boys called it quits, and the shark swam away. Leave a shark alone. They have a right to be here too."

Ansil pulled up to the mouth of a mangrove creek. He'd stopped here many years ago, he told us, with Dr. Martin Luther King Jr. "He didn't come here to fish. He came to write. He was preparing his speech to accept the Nobel Prize and wanted to be inspired by the beauty of nature. I took him to this place, right here. I tied the boat up and we sat here for two hours, looking at the clouds, the sky, the little fishes moving in the water. It was so beautiful he had tears in his eyes."

In April 1968, King came back for a second trip in Ansil's boat. This time he was composing a speech supporting a garbage workers' strike in Memphis. Shortly afterward, King went to Memphis and was shot, allegedly by James Earl Ray. Ansil was so devastated by the murder that he decided to organize a desegregation campaign in King's honor.

He picked one of the bastions of white supremacy—the Bimini Big Game Fishing Club. "Every hotel on the island was the same, no black people allowed. I went in there every day and sat down for lunch, and nobody served me. I'd sit there for an hour, and they wouldn't come to my table. They didn't ask me to leave. They just ignored me. After an hour I'd get up and go out on the water again. They knew I was hungry. It was hot outside, and they wouldn't even give me a glass of water. Finally they must have felt sorry for me, because they took my order and brought me lunch. Once they served me, all the other hotels gave up and agreed to serve me too. Now a black person can go into any business in the Bahamas and ask for service. People think there's always been equal rights, and that black people are just troublemakers. But we had to fight for every single right we have. Those old white boys wanted to keep the whole island for themselves."

Back at the pier, we gave Ansil a nice tip and thanked him for a great day of fishing. When we returned to the cabin I climbed out of my dirty pants and decided I'd walk down to the beach for a swim. We had to leave the next morning, and I wanted to commune with the ocean one more time. While I was changing, Paul went out into the yard and asked the laundry lady if she'd ever heard of a big white house that Hemingway once lived in. "Why yes sir," she said. "That's it right there." She was pointing at the house next door to our cabin.

"Hey Jakey," Paul chuckled as I came out to join him. "We finally found it."

We looked at the neighboring house, about fifteen yards away. It was a big white clapboard house, all right, old and solid, with a second-floor balcony and big windows overlooking the sea. Down below the house was the clean, pure-white sand beach where the fictional Thomas Hudson and the real Ernest Hemingway had taken their swims every morning.

At the bottom of the stairs I threw my towel on the sand and went into the water. I swam out until I could feel a faint coolness, the first hint of the abyss. Another three or four hundred yards and I'd reach that purple line that marked the edge of the Gulf Stream.

That evening P.Q. and I walked down to the Compleat Angler for a few drinks. It was a hot night, with thunder booming over the ocean. You could hear the calypso music coming out the door. The place was crowded, full of young Americans who'd just gotten off a boat. Paul and I sat at the bar, drinking banana-flavored cocktails with little umbrellas in them. Hemingway and his cronies smiled down at us from the wall.

||||||||||||||||||||||||||||||||||||||||||||||||||||

Roughing It
IN THE BUSH

◇◇◇◇◇

*I*n the winter I live in the city, where there's very little contact with Nature. Any unauthorized animal in my house is, by definition, vermin, and is subject to fatwa, an immediate death sentence. This fatwa especially applies to insects. Centipedes lurk under the damp towels in my basement laundry bin, and this offends me. Rodents? I hate them, and I'm a liberal. Recently, my sister Mary Kate saw a mouse in her living room and announced that she was selling her house. That's the way it is, in the city. But as soon as ice-out arrives in the spring, I start spending time at my houseboat in Minaki, and the balance of power tips dramatically in favor of the critters. When I'm at the houseboat, they own the place.

When naturalists are studying a piece of wildlife habitat, one of the first things they do is count the residents. It would be interesting to conduct the same sort of study at the average lake-country cottage. How many hornets live in that nest under the eaves? How many spiders inhabit the crannies along the windows? Most of us couldn't identify these organisms, let alone count them. In bed at night, open-eyed in the darkness, I listen to the drone of mosquitoes, the scamper of feet, the flutter of wings, and I feel like Gulliver, lying on my back in the middle of some swarming Lilliputian city.

I may not be personally acquainted with my neighbors, but I've learned to recognize the sound of their comings and goings. Mice make a light patter as they run across the roof. Muskrats make a fishy splash as they hunt for food among the cattails. A much louder splash, followed by a clunk of wood, means a beaver has arrived, hauling a piece of cut aspen. And if there's a clean, efficient plop in the water, followed by dead silence from all the other residents, it means that the mink has arrived. He's the one who ruins the party, our own local version of Mack the Knife.

I rarely see the mink, but I find his handiwork. He leaves the doll-like feet of young rabbits on the shore and the backbones of perch and rock bass on my front deck. If you leave a minnow bucket tied to the side of the boat or to the swimming ladder, it's usually empty in the morning. Somehow the mink manages to push open the spring-loaded trapdoor and nab the minnows one by one. I'm glad he can do it without getting caught. I'd rather not think about stuffing my hand into a minnow bucket with a miniature meat grinder waiting inside.

It's hard to believe, but mink can even get into latched storage compartments. One night I came home from fishing with a plump eighteen-inch walleye that I planned to have for breakfast. It was nightfall, too late to clean the fish, so I left it in my boat's live well, a metal compartment with an electric pump inside that keeps it charged with fresh water. I checked to make sure the walleye was still swimming, then closed the lid and fastened its complicated chrome latch. The next morning, the lid was still latched, but the live well was empty. I'm not saying that the mink unfastened the latch. I'm just saying the fish was gone.

Toward the end of summer, the population of my little metropolis takes a sharp decline. The nights grow colder, and the leaves begin to turn. The insects die off and the bats disappear too, migrating to wherever bats go in the wintertime. Every summer, a perky little pair of phoebes raise a brood under the roof overhang. Now, according to my bird book, they're headed two thousand miles south, to the Gulf of Mexico. The chubby juvenile beaver who has spent the summer thumping around in my undercarriage finally realizes that my houseboat won't suffice as winter housing. So he too hits the trail. Every morning, you look around and notice that another creature has departed. It's an exodus. As Joni Mitchell noted, those who stay are dying, and those who live are getting out.

Only the mink hangs around. He's made of tough stuff. In another few months, the ice will be four feet thick. The snow will be piled thigh-deep in the woods, and the north wind will freeze your eyelids shut in half a second. But the mink doesn't care. He looks downright jaunty as he canters along the shore. I begin to see him regularly. I feel like telling him what Richard Boone said to Paul Newman in the movie *Hombre,* "You've got some hard bark on you, mister." His fur has grown thick and glossy. And when he stands up to look me over, revealing that distinctive white chuck-mark under his jaw, he has the fearless aspect of a pure predator. It's obvious that he'd like to fasten his teeth in my cervical vertebrae. He's just not sure if he can take me or not.

On Remembrance Day, I sometimes drive to the lake to haul my boat out of the water and bring in cans of paint, soup

53

and other liquids that can't be left at the houseboat all winter. My sister Mary Kate's husband, John Harvie, has chores of his own to do, so we sometimes make the trip together. John is not a backwoodsman. He's an urbane fellow, a fan of obscure Hollywood musicals and evening wear. His boat is a gleaming wooden cruiser bedecked with chrome sirens and flags, and he comes with me on these Remembrance Day trips so that he can tuck his own boat away for the winter.

Like any good nostalgia buff, John tends to believe that most of the greatest music, art, and films were made before we were born. Because it's Remembrance Day, our conversations are usually tinged by nostalgia. As we drive past the khaki fields and forests we talk about war, movies, and the way we imagine things used to be. Sometimes we discuss our latest screenplay project. We always have a screenplay project underway. These screenplays never get produced, but we keep writing them anyway. John is the most film-literate person I've met. He's done some acting, and he once played the starring role in a picture by Winnipeg film director Guy Maddin. But he doesn't like the word "film" because it's pretentious, and he doesn't like the word "movie" because it's low-brow. He likes to refer to them as "pictures." Often, when we're trying to figure out how to frame a scene in our latest picture, he'll say something like: "It's like the bugle scene in *Road to Glory*."

"That Mel Gibson movie?"

"No, you idiot."

"Refresh my memory."

"Written in 1935 by William Faulkner, starring Lionel Barrymore and Warner Baxter?"

"I don't believe I've seen it."

"How can you call yourself a writer when you haven't seen *Road to Glory*?"

"Tell me the scene."

"Barrymore plays the father. He's lied about his age to fight alongside his son, and he's brought this bugle he carried in the Sudan."

"Okay."

As John describes the story, the austere landscape rolls by. At eleven o'clock the radio takes us to the nation's capital, where the rattle of drums and the mournful wail of the bugle salute the fallen soldiers of the great wars. The bitterly cold wind tearing at my cracked-open wind vent reminds me that we don't belong in this country. This country is spiraling down into winter, a season ruled by grim little warriors like the mink.

I grew up in the city, in one of those postwar neighborhoods with rows of identical tract houses and boulevard trees the size of hockey sticks. When I was five years old my parents gave me and my six brothers and sisters a gift. They bought a vacant lot at a place called Lulu Lake, and upon that weedy lot they built a cottage. It was my first experience with nature; not the "World of Nature" as seen on *Walt Disney Presents,* with cute bunnies and harmonizing bluebirds, but the majestic and frightening wilderness. The one that makes you feel as insignificant as a gnat.

At the local beach on our lake there was a swimming platform, and if you got exhausted swimming out to it, you were on your own. One kid didn't make it. The ambulance came and took him away, and that was the end of that. I'd always suspected that life was cruel, beneath all the grown-up fibs and platitudes, and although Nature was terrifying I loved her authenticity. The goddess of Nature was an Old Testament deity. She had no rewards for anyone who couldn't look into her cold and beautiful face. The forests, the waters, and

55

the creeping animals of creation were the first real evidence I'd encountered of something bigger and scarier than what I'd known before. All winter, in the city, I thought about the lake: its look, its smell, the tools that you needed to live there.

Having a knack for backwoods living is a point of pride for many Canadians. We might live in the city, but we like to think we know how to pitch a tent or clean a fish. One of my female friends used to audition boyfriends by taking them to her family's cottage, where she'd put them through their paces to see if they met the minimum standards. She fired one fellow after only a day or two; something to do with a fear of water. She was so appalled she couldn't bother taking him to the train station. Her brother did the deed. The rejected suitor was from Colorado, so he had an excuse for not knowing how to swim, but he should have known better than to date a woman from Canada.

When I first met John Harvie, I was similarly skeptical of his backwoods skills. I was newly divorced, living with my four-year-old daughter Caitlin in a rambling old apartment in Winnipeg. One night my sister offered to babysit so that I could go to a movie. When I returned, I discovered an interloper in my living room. He had slicked-back hair and was wearing a summer suit with a gold watch chain hanging from the vest. If I'd owned a farm, I would have assumed that he'd shown up to repossess it.

John understood that he was on probation with Mary Kate, so for a short time he worked hard at winning my approval. When Mary Kate followed the local practice and brought him to the lake for his inevitable tryout, I stood on the dock watching them approach in a rented boat. John, dressed in a blazer, turtleneck, and jaunty yachting cap, failed the docking test when he shut off the motor prematurely, swung the tiller hard to port, and ended up floating dead in the water a good five feet away from the dock. Flushed with embarrassment, he yanked the cord of the motor. But now, with witnesses on the scene, it wouldn't start. My sister sat in the bow with the boxes of groceries, pretending to be preoccupied with the beauty of Nature. Muttering an apology, John threw me a rope. It fell in the water. He looked at the gap between us, trying to maintain a minimum level of dignity. "Just jump," I suggested.

He vaulted from the boat. He didn't make it even halfway to the dock. He hit the lake with a great splash, and for a long moment there was nothing on the water but his floating hat. Finally he surfaced.

"I was kidding," I said.

Despite his so-so performance at the tiller, my sister agreed to marry him. I gave the toast to the bride, and their marriage ended the brief and happy power imbalance between John and me. We are now peers who take turns abusing each other. Actually, he abuses me. I'm no match for him. He has become a skilled boat handler, and sometimes I have to admit that his antique wooden boat looks to be in better shape than mine. With the passing of my father, Mary Kate and John have taken on a major role in maintaining the cottage at Lulu Lake. When John and I make our ritualistic trip on Remembrance Day, we stop first at Lulu Lake to put his boat away, then carry on to Minaki to deal with mine.

When the chores are finished, if we have time, we go fishing. It's always terribly cold, but if you're gritty enough, walleye fishing is often at its best in early November. Baitfish, insects, and crustaceans have died off, and the walleyes attack anything that resembles food. Last year, we cruised around the corner to a swampy bay that usually provides

57

some good late-autumn fishing. We were wearing mitts and winter parkas. With the sun on our faces, it was hard to guess the temperature, but the boat's cotton ropes were frozen stiff. As soon as we started to fish, tendrils of ice congealed on the tips of our fishing rods.

The fish were very hungry. They snapped hard at our baits, fought stubbornly, and looked so pretty, coming up out of the dark water, that I hated to kill a few for dinner. When we got back to the houseboat, it was so cold and gloomy inside, with the windows boarded up, that we cooked outside on the barbecue. We heaped our plates with pan-fried potatoes, onions, green peppers, beans, tinned corn, and big slabs of walleye. The plates steamed in the cold. The sun was getting lower, and it felt good to get the hot food inside us. We were just getting involved in a second helping when John pointed. "Hey, look at the beaver."

The mink climbed up on the deck and shook himself off. He was wearing a fine, glossy robe of winter fur, and he eyed us without a trace of fear. "You'd better not let Yvonne De Carlo see you in that coat," John said.

The mink was in no mood for small talk. He organized and stockpiled the fish scraps while we ate. He dragged each backbone into the water, then swam around to the back of the houseboat and stuffed them into a half-submerged hollow log, where I suppose he thought they'd be safe from freeloaders. He seized the skins, one by one, then galloped up onto the island and buried them at the base of a tree.

58   After fifteen minutes, only the entrails remained. He dragged them up and down the rocks for a few minutes, then decided to hide them in the undercarriage of the houseboat. It took him the better part of half an hour to complete all these chores. When he was finished, he loped off down

the shore in pursuit of other errands. He was perhaps fifty
yards away when he suddenly stopped and stood still, as if a
thought had just occurred to him.

He came loping back, hauled a skeleton out of the hollow
log, climbed up onto the deck of the houseboat, and started
chewing. He started at one end of the skeleton and gnawed
his way along as if it were a cob of corn. We watched him for
a while. Then the sun went down, and it began to get seriously cold. Washing our plates in the lake, we cleaned up and
then started loading the boat with my boxes of tinned goods.
The mink kept eating. He wasn't the least bit afraid. We had
to skirt around him as we worked.

Finally, the boat was packed. I did one final check on the
houseboat and then padlocked the door. What a sad moment
this always is. Winters are long in this country, and if you're
realistic you have to accept that you might never see the
place again. I climbed into the boat, fired up the motor, and
untied the frozen ropes. The exhaust from the engine rolled
like fog across the still water. Freeze-up was coming, maybe
even tonight.

The mink trotted along the deck and licked a splash of
blood off the wood. I gave the motor a bit of gas. He was so
close I could have touched him, and he didn't look at us as we
drove away.

||||||||||||||||||||||||||||||||||||||||||||||||||||||

Conversations

WITH CHARLIE

◇◇◇◇◇

I first met Charles Wilkins at a book launch, when we were rookie writers who had contributed short stories to the same anthology. Charles was the first "real" writer I'd ever met, in the sense that he had no job other than writing. I had recently returned to the city, after a long stint living in the backwoods, and I sensed that Charles was a few moves ahead of me. I liked the cut of his jib, especially when he got up on stage and gave an extemporaneous and very funny speech. We got into a conversation after the party, and we've been talking regularly ever since.

Charles loves talking. On occasion we have taken long motor trips, and on the first day of the journey it usually eats up three or four hours just to work our way through the introductory part of the conversation. I've always thought of our friendship as a kind of script, in which Charles plays the monologist and I play the friendly ear, but he would no doubt disagree. Once, for example, while we were heading for Montreal on an icy, black night with snowflakes bombing through the headlights, he glanced at me, with a slight expression of exasperation, and said, "Don't you ever shut up?"

This sporadic, decades-long conversation has produced many side effects. One day I was having lunch with Charles and mentioned that I'd agreed to undertake a twelve-hundred-mile, eight-stop tour of northern Manitoba, meeting with local writing groups. The idea of spending two weeks on the road in the far north kind of tuckered me out, however, so I asked Charlie if he wanted to split the money and the responsibilities. Naturally, I offered him the farthest towns.

Keen for the income, he rented a car and headed north. Manitoba's Highway 6 goes for hundreds of miles through the northern muskeg. The road is featureless and deserted and straight as a knife cut. The landscape is so monotonous that you have to guzzle coffee and drive with the radio at high volume or you'll fall asleep and crash into a tree. As Charles tells it, he was going 110 miles an hour when a timber wolf stepped onto the highway ahead of him. He tapped the brakes. A mile away, an RCMP officer caught him on the radar gun at 98 mph. When the cop stopped him, Charles said, "Gosh, I'm sorry, constable, but can't you give me a break on this?"

"I am giving you a break," the cop said. "Good thing you weren't going two miles an hour faster or I'd have to put you in jail."

Saved by the wolf, Charles pressed on to the mining town of Leaf Rapids, where he gave a reading. One of the members of the audience was an attractive young woman named Betty Carpick. She was an artist and writer who made a decent buck working at the local Ruttan Mine. After the reading, Betty stayed to chat with Charles and buy one of his books.

Charles was having some problems with his relationship back home—the last time he'd seen his girlfriend she was chasing him down the sidewalk with an Econoline van—and Betty, although she was with her boyfriend, was interested enough to accept Charles's offer to accompany him upstairs so he could "sign her book." In his room, Charles turned on the charm, chatting with Betty about this and that, while her boyfriend, down in the parking lot below, kept throwing snowballs at the window. A few months later, thanks to my laziness, they were living together.

Charles and I like dissecting our favorite books, trying to figure out why they work so well. (Elmore Leonard once suggested, "Leave out the boring parts.") On a whim, one December, we decided to drive from Toronto to Vermont to visit Edward Hoagland. Most people have never heard of Hoagland, but Charles and I had been poring over his books for years and had concluded he was just about the best writer alive. On the pretext of interviewing him for some literary magazine, I'd hounded Hoagland by mail. Finally, employing a crabbed and childlike scrawl, he'd sent me a postcard agreeing to a visit at his home. After stocking up on taped music and road snacks, Charles and I gassed up his old Nova and headed off.

Vermont isn't far from Toronto as the crow flies, but we weren't crows. It took us two days to get there. I passed the time by turning on the dome light and reading some of our favorite sections from Hoagland's books. When the road got too bouncy to read we gabbed about this and that, argued and laughed; smoked cigarettes and criticized people who in our opinion deserved a run of bad luck. Late at night, we finally arrived in the town of Bennington, home of the great one. At a cheap motel near Bennington College, where Hoagland taught, we hauled our bags up to our second-floor room, where we had a dinner of Coke and potato chips and flipped through late-night TV.

The next day, at five o'clock in the afternoon, we rang his doorbell, and Edward Hoagland, aged sixty-one, loped to the door. He was a tall, strong-looking man in thick eye-glasses and a moth-eaten beige cardigan of the sort fathers and uncles seem to like. He was wearing muddy loafers and a rumpled old fedora. He looked as if we'd interrupted him in the middle of some yard work. "Come in," he said, with a stut-ter. "I'm w-w-watching the news."

We went into his living room and sat down on the couch. Hoagland sat on an ottoman in front of the television and studied the NBC news. He didn't speak or even look at us. As ten minutes turned into fifteen minutes, and then half an hour, it seemed increasingly bizarre that he'd invited us into his home and was now staring at the television without saying a word. Charles and I exchanged concerned glances.

Finally, when NBC had wrung out every drop of news, Hoagland stood up and, with a glottal constriction in his throat, stammered, "Should we g-g-go and eat?"

We drove downtown and had dinner in a Chinese res-taurant. I took out the tape recorder, turned it on, tested it, placed it delicately on the table between us, and posed the first of the questions that Charles and I had spent the last two days composing. Feeling too nervous to eat, I picked at my dinner. Hoagie, as Charles and I were privately in the habit of calling him, eyed my plate like a starving hobo. Half-way through one of my questions—one of those long-winded, self-absorbed questions that young writers love to construct— he reached across the table and speared one of my breaded shrimp, popped it in his mouth and chewed ferociously. I told

63

him that in his essays, one couldn't help noticing that the world, as he rendered it, was more intense, more dramatic, more multidimensional, more *surprising* than the beaten-up old shoe of a world that most of us walked around in. Was he gifted with an extraordinary clarity of sight? Or did he just work harder on his writing?

"The s-second one," he replied. "I work h-h-harder on the writing."

He speared another shrimp and then, with great care, wrapped my baked potato in a paper napkin and slipped it into his pocket. He explained that he'd bummed around the world for years, hitchhiking, hopping freighters, sleeping on the ground, and couldn't bear to watch food going to waste. I asked him more questions, about his days working in the circus, his travels in the Antarctic, in Africa, and in northern British Columbia, chronicled in the brilliant journal *Notes from the Century Before*. He answered with scrupulous modesty, scowling for a moment before stammering a reply. He seemed to assume that Charles and I were accomplished writers in our own communities and had tramped the world as much as he had. Had we been to Namibia? Had we been to that wonderful opera house in Manaus, Brazil? No, we said, we hadn't been anywhere.

The interview lasted for several hours. Hoagland struggled stubbornly with his speech impediment, a stutter so severe that at times he fought for air. It seemed divinely cruel that the man whom John Updike once dubbed "the finest essayist in the English language" would have to work so hard at ordinary conversation. But as Charles pointed out on our drive back to Canada the next day, maybe Hoagland's affliction offered certain compensations. He couldn't talk, but he could write like Roy Orbison could sing.

When Charles and I crossed the line into Canada, we checked into another motel, where we decided to listen to Hoagie's interview on tape. We popped open a couple of beers and sat on our beds, listening to the hum of the tape recorder, waiting for the great man to speak. As a final joke on us, the tape was blank.

CHARLES AND I HAVE embarked other adventures. I've tried to introduce him to fishing and hunting, but most of our adventures have been unsuccessful. Charlie takes pleasure in recounting the time I took him duck hunting on a large, placid-looking pond that turned out to be a sewage lagoon. We actually bagged a couple of ducks, but when Charles took them home and cooked them, the oven threw off such a foul odor that he and his family had to clear the house.

I also regaled him with tales of fishing in Mexico. After several years of hemming and hawing on his part, we finally coordinated a trip to Barra de Navidad, a village on the Pacific coast. I've gone there many times and regard it as my southern version of Minaki. Charles arrived with his wife, kids, and mother-in-law—what Zorba the Greek called "the full catastrophe." After a few days of relaxing, swimming, and sun-tanning with his family, Charles felt he'd be able to slip away for a morning of fishing.

Fishing is one of those sports in which the lead-up is as pleasurable as the actual experience. Ostensibly you're going out to catch a few nice ones for lunch. But the adventure begins in the darkness of early morning, when the alarm goes off and you lie in bed for a few minutes listening to the sound of the sea piling in against the beach. That morning, slipping out of bed, I left my girlfriend folded in luscious sleep and tip-toed into the bathroom to get dressed. Gathering my knapsack and fishing rods, careful to avoid introducing their delicate tips to the spinning ceiling fan, I padded down the concrete stairs to the lobby. The front desk was still closed and Jorge the night manager was still in dreamland, snuffling like a hog, chin down on his chest, with his fingers laced across his gut and the black handle of the unobtrusive little .25 automatic protruding from the belt of his dress slacks. I slipped past him, out into the cobblestone street. The sky was just beginning to lighten, and except for the distant skirl of a rooster the village was pin-drop silent.

Charles was standing in front of the only shop in town that was open. He had purchased some bread, bottled water, and half a dozen bananas for our breakfast. He was dressed informally for our fishing trip—rubber flip-flops, a well-faded denim shirt, and a beat-up old straw hat that looked like it had once belonged to Mister Ed. Charles is the sort of old-school bohemian writer whose caffeine-fueled all-nighters sometimes don't start until 10 or 11 PM, so it was unusual to see him looking so chipper at this hour. He gestured at my fishing rods. "You brought one for me?"

"Yes, sir, we're ready to go."

As we walked down through the village, women were emerging from their shacks and sweeping the cobblestones. There's no other place in the world that has an aroma like Barra de Navidad in the early morning. It's a blend of sea air, fish, charcoal smoke, and tropical flowers. Still blurry-eyed from sleep, picking up my feet to avoid tripping on the uneven cobblestones, I thought I should open a jar and pass it through the humid darkness, capturing the smell so that on wintry mornings up north I could take a whiff and be transported back to this scene.

When we arrived at the docks, the fishermen were organizing their boats. Across the silvery lagoon the eastern sky was turning pink. My guide and old friend Luis Canela was already on duty, attending to his ancient Yamaha motor. Luis spends almost every day working on the ocean. I've known him since he was the village's handsome young Romeo, fourteen years old. He's now a hardworking fisherman with a family of his own, but he still has a boyish awe of the world around him. Early in the morning, when you meet him at the lagoon and climb into his boat, he smiles and quietly makes the sign of the cross before he starts his engine. When you kid him about whether he's praying for good fishing, he laughs and shakes his head. "God will take care of you when you're on the ocean," he says in Spanish. "But you have to catch the fish by yourself."

Charles and I had been taking Spanish lessons from Lolize, the smart and pretty young woman who managed our hotel. Lolize comported herself with the haughty demeanor of a Castilian princess and liked to make sport with guys like me. When I came in late at night and asked her if I could have my room key, she would glance at me, blithely say, "No," and go back to reading her movie star magazine.

Her make-do classroom was a hotel balcony. We sat there on wooden chairs and scribbled our assignments in our notebooks while the surf roared below. No one was allowed to speak English. "Most men are stupid and lazy," Lolize instructed.

We were supposed to write this down in Spanish.

Charles wrote feverishly, then handed her his notebook. "In my country," Charles recited in Spanish, "men get respect from women."

Lolize scratched a large red X through his sentence. "Yes, but now you are in Mexico."

The Mexican version of the Spanish language is complicated by all kinds of colloquialisms and regional sayings, and although I can usually handle the language well enough

67

to keep the conversation bouncing uncertainly back and forth, Luis occasionally serves up an offhand that catches me flat-footed.

For example, one morning he explained that he was late because "a Brahma bull stepped on my friend's head." I asked him for details but got lost, in short order, in the tangled pluperfects and subjunctives that entrap amateurish second-language speakers anytime they wander beyond the simple Grade Five–level declarative narrative. Was he describing a gruesome death or just a bad hangover?

Climbing into Luis's boat, Charles and I stowed our gear. Luis started the engine. It sounded like a jerry can full of nails and sent billowing clouds of blue smoke across the water. Luis untied the bow rope and raised the anchor. Using my bunched-up windbreaker, I wiped the dew off the seats and sat down, unscrewed the cap on a bottle of orange juice, and took a sip. Luis backed away from the pier. It's impossible to describe the beauty of that moment: the glassy lagoon, the roseate glow of the eastern sky, and the gassy reek of the drifting engine exhaust—a smell that since childhood I've associated with the beauty of nature. The pelicans, too, were heading off to sea, and they flapped alongside us like low-flying bomber escorts, their images perfectly mirrored on the water.

Past the lagoon entrance, the boat climbed the first gentle swell of the open sea. The ocean was as smooth as a meadow, and the orange sun was bulging over the horizon. *Tijeras*, or frigate birds, wheeled overhead, their scissor tails flaring as they drifted on the early thermals. Luis was standing on the back seat with his arms folded, steering the tiller with his bare foot. Smiling at us, he shouted a request. *"Puedo cantar?"*

"Por cierto, amigo."

68

Luis sang, his voice lifting over the drone of the outboard. Luis is well into his thirties, but he's still got the heart of a boy. In his adolescence he worked as a skin diver, diving for lobsters. He can hold his breath for two minutes. One year the police asked him for help because a sailboat had sunk offshore with an American yachtsman on board. The police wanted Luis to dive down and tie a rope to the body so that they could pull it up. "I told them no," he said. "It would make me too sad."

Luis quit working as a diver because it was damaging his heart. He moved to Los Angeles for a while but didn't like it. The Americans think that every working-class Mexican can't wait to sneak across the border, but Luis has told me that he loves living in this village.

As we surged across the waves, I opened my tackle box and sorted through my lures. Charles watched me tie the lure onto his line, and when I handed him the rod he grinned as if I'd given him a birthday present. Holding the rod upright between his knees, he went back to studying the birds and the high cliffs going past. His head swiveled like a dashboard puppy's.

Our first stop was a craggy reef that local fishermen call the *Viejo.* The tide was running hard, pulling line off our reels as soon as our lures hit the water. It was difficult to get the lures down into the deep sheltered pockets where the fish lived. After an hour's work I'd caught nothing but a dappled rockfish the Mexicans call a *pantillo,* a "painted one," which I released on the grounds that it was too pretty and too small to kill. Charles made a wry comment as I flipped the wee creature into the ocean. Moving on, we tried another good spot, a bay called the Bahia del Coco. The waves were sloshing against the cliffs and the place looked fishy enough, but

69

frigate birds and boobies were snoozing on the rocks. When the birds can't be bothered fishing, that's the first clue you're wasting your time.

By ten-thirty in the morning the sun was uncomfortably hot. We lathered our arms with a fresh helping of sunblock and sat back in our seats, tugging our hats down low. The breeze was rising, and the heaving waves were developing frothy crowns of foam and spray. When the boat struck a wave crosswise the salt water came splattering back in the wind, a nice feeling in the heat. I poured some cold drinking water onto my red bandanna and knotted the deliciously chilly rag around my neck. I wordlessly handed the plastic bottle of drinking water to Charles, and he wordlessly drank from it.

Charles seemed to be enjoying himself. But I was determined to catch some fish. Luis likewise looked concerned. As we bounced across the waves, he searched for diving birds or swarming baitfish to indicate the presence of fish. Cruising north for three miles, we finally reached a place called *Las Iglesias,* The Cathedrals. The rocks here are as large as medieval churches, and heavy green swells crash and echo among them. At the base of one cliff, a blowhole sucks in the huge waves and shoots them out in a blast of spray. Ducking through a narrow passage, Luis steered the boat through a quiet alleyway. The water was turquoise green, so transparent that we could see moray eels and octopi crawling among the rocks far below.

As we cruised along, we looked into the aquamarine depths and scrutinized the cliffs above us. Birds wheeled overhead. The ocean was heaving under us, and we were dead silent, taking it all in. I've often thought that I'd like to have my ashes scattered here. It's the most beautiful place I've ever seen. At the end of the alleyway, the cliffs opened up and we

70

were once again riding the high swell into the open sea. As Luis gunned the motor, he pointed across the heaving waves. "Sierra," he exclaimed.

The creatures of the ocean operate by invisible rhythms. For some reason, all the birds, baitfish, and predators in the neighborhood had decided it was time to eat. A hundred yards ahead of us, dozens of pelicans were diving into the sea. Panicked sardines were spattering out of the waves. Fins and wide tails slashed the water all around them. Sierra mackerel are fast and aggressive predators with mouths full of razor teeth. We cast simultaneously. Our metal sardine lures hit the water and, instantly, Charles was hooked up. His reel screamed as a sierra seized his lure and took off. A moment later, my line started thumping, as if someone was beating it with a stick.

"Gee haw!" shouted Luis, grinning. "Two of them!"

We landed both fish, a couple of four-pounders with leopard-spotted slippery skins that threw off flashes of blue and green iridescence. Charlie's was a bit larger. It tried to bite Luis as he removed the hook. As beautiful as this place is, it's a boiler room of brute survival. Every creature in the ocean is either killing or about to get killed. Luis delicately removed the hook and slapped the fish on the head with a wooden billy. He dropped it into the shade beneath his boat seat. I unhooked mine and tossed it back into the ocean; one four-pounder was enough for lunch. We kept fishing, caught and released three more sierra, and then I gave Luis the thumbs-up. "Okay, *compadre, basta por hoy.*"

He nodded, and we headed back for town. By the time we got to Barra it was almost noon. Temperature differential between land and ocean was driving hot air toward the shore, and the palms were rattling fiercely in the strong wind. Four or five hours on the ocean beats you up. It was nice to get

71

back on dry land and make our way along the shady side of the street. My shirt was dirty and stiff with salt. In the hotel room, I kicked off my sandals and turned on the shower.

Along Avenida Miguel Lopez de Legazpi, there's a fabulous little grass-thatched restaurant called Ramón's. Ramón and his family work day and night, preparing seafood meals that some people regard as the best eating on the entire coast of Jalisco. Ramón is an artist of the charcoal grill, and his long refrigerator is filled with chipped ice and fresh lobster, whole grouper, red snapper, octopus, dorado, and whatever else the sea is offering that day.

When fishermen like Charles and me show up, hauling our fish, Ramón always makes a great welcoming fuss. He is quick with a filleting knife. Only a few minutes after we sat down, his handsome son Juan Pablo, a medical student, came to our table with a platter of frijoles, rice, corn tortillas, hot sauce, and grilled sierra.

Perfect. When you eat at Ramón's, your meal comes with a shady thatch overhead, a cold glass of beer, and a view of the ocean. Polishing off our lunch, Charles and I scrutinized the white sand and the strolling swimmers. Wiping my hands with the cloth napkin, I leaned back in my chair. I cleaned my sunglasses and watched the turquoise waves bursting onto the beach. Charles sat with his hands laced across his knee, moving only to take an occasional sip of beer. Usually we'd be yakking by now, swapping tips and making business plans. But we'd never come up with a better plan than this. So we just sat there enjoying the moment, silent for a change.

|||||||||||||||||||||||||||||||||||||||||||||||||||||||

A *Relaxing*
TRIP TO
THE BARREN LANDS

◇◇◇◇◇

It's a warm summer day on the Barren Lands, and I'm sitting alone in the cockpit of a $1 million French A-Star helicopter. Through the polished lenses of my sleek Ray-Ban sunglasses, I can see the quiver and twitch of a dozen high-tech instruments monitoring the various functions of the thundering engines. The high-pitched pulsing of the rotors, the trembling of the airframe, and the chattering scream of the turbines all attest to the fact that the helicopter is primed for takeoff.

It's impossible to sit inside a helicopter without feeling a mix of exhilaration and dread. Rookie chopper pilots spend an inordinate amount of time learning the simplest maneuvers, like raising the thing a few inches off the ground and trying to keep it there. Airplanes want to fly, and helicopters want to somersault and slap themselves to pieces. Judging by its near-hysterical vocalizations, this machine is ready to get

started. The pilot is outside. He and my companions are loading luggage into the rear compartment. The pilot has given me
the okay to get strapped in. He didn't say, "By the way, don't
touch any of the controls." I guess he thought I was smart
enough to know that.

The sexy A-Star has 360-degree visibility and a cockpit
composed entirely of Plexiglas. Looking down through my
feet I can see the low carpet of berry bushes buffeting in the
rotor blast. I pull on the bulky headphones, and the thick rubber seals cut the engine noise down to a muffled thudding.
Groping in the space between the seats, I locate the metal
seat belt bracket. Running my hand along the bar, I twist and
pull, trying to free the belt. Instantly, the engine's RPMs begin
to accelerate. Oh boy, I guess that wasn't the seat belt bracket
after all. The helicopter starts shuddering. I realize, with a
sense of horror, that it's going to lift off.

When something very bad is about to happen, time slows
down. Each millisecond clicks past frame by frame. I can
see every detail of what's coming. The machine will rise. The
wind will tip it over to the right. The rotor will whack into the
tundra, and the tail rotor will sweep into my friends. Gyrating
wildly, the helicopter will begin beating itself to death, kicking body parts and red spray in all directions. I realize, with
gravity, that this is the worst screw-up I've ever committed.
To make things worse, when the machine is finished tearing
itself apart, I'll probably still be alive.

74   TOM THOMSON is an outdoor photographer. He and I had
always wanted to visit the Barren Lands. So, after a few sum-
mers of thinking it over, I called a northern outfitter named
Keith Sharp and asked him if he had any suggestions.

Keith Sharp grew up in northern England, and when you
talk to him over an echoing satellite telephone he sounds like

Willy the Groundskeeper yelling from the bottom of a well. He explained that the tourist season was pretty well over, but he needed to go out to his cabin on the banks of the Kazan River and do some chores and close it for the winter. If Tom and I could find our way to Rankin Inlet, we were welcome to come up and join him for the four days he planned to spend there.

This was our chance. A few days later, on a hot afternoon in late August, we boarded a Calm Air flight from Winnipeg to Rankin Inlet. Tom brought along a knapsack full of photographic gear. At this time of year, the antlers of the caribou would still be in velvet, and he was especially hoping for a close-up shot of a big bull. I was hoping to catch a big lake trout on my fly rod.

The flight was full of government workers, teachers, and nurses, all of whom seemed to relax noticeably as the plane gained cruising altitude. Even in this modern era, traveling north feels like an adventure, and the passengers were as animated as a group of grade-seven students on a fieldtrip. They wandered up and down the aisle, drinking beer and yakking. The pretty, uniformed flight attendant kicked off her high heels and carried out her duties in her stockings. We stopped in Churchill ("Polar Bear Capital of the World!"), then forged on to the town of Rankin Inlet, which sits on the northwestern shore of Hudson Bay. By the time we landed the weather had turned gray and blustery.

Keith Sharp had promised to meet us at the airport, but he was nowhere to be seen. Tom and I hailed a taxi and rode through Rankin, a mostly disastrous maze of prefab metal buildings, gravel streets, and rusty vehicles. Near the middle of town, at the end of a rough road lined with barking dogs and snowmobiles, we checked into the Sinniktarvik, the town's largest and only hotel. After we got settled, we called Keith's house. No answer.

Tom and I shrugged off the missing Keith and headed out to explore the town. Rankin Inlet (population 2,200) is built on bare rock, and the houses are scattered like abandoned packing crates. Each house looks as if it's hosting an apocalyptic garage sale. The yards are cluttered with gutted sofas, wooden pallets, discarded septic tanks, car bodies, dismantled snowmobiles, dried hides, and the bleached vertebral columns and shoulder blades of assorted dead mammals. Tiny fat children clamber and vault from the wreckage. The local Inuit kids are ridiculously cute, with dark, almond-shaped eyes and open, trusting faces. Everywhere we went, they yelped and waved at us.

Down at the harbor, we spotted three young Inuit guys pulling a boat up on the beach. They were dirty and tough-looking. If they'd been walking down a street in South Central L.A., people would have stepped out of their way. But urban stereotypes didn't apply to these guys. They waved at us, with big smiles, and we walked down to say hello. It turned out that they were dirty because they'd been living in the boat for three days. And they didn't have to act tough, because they were. They told us they'd been out hunting whales. Their equipment was an eclectic mix of old and new. They were carrying rifles with rangefinder scopes and stainless steel barrels. The boat contained a couple of massive, rusty old harpoons, and their big stainless steel Coleman cooler was full of greasy hunks of muktuq—raw whale blubber. "One whale will keep the three of us in meat all winter," one of them said. Belugas weigh nine hundred pounds, four hundred of which is meat. But the challenge is to get close enough to hit one with a harpoon, then kill it with the rifles.

The three hunters said the whales had been spooky and hard to approach. When darkness fell each night, they anchored in the lee of a white quartz island and crawled under the bow to sleep. "It's a lot of work to kill a whale," one of them said. "They hear the motor coming, they take off. They're wild whales. They aren't like those tame whales you guys have in the zoo."

By the time we got back to the hotel, Keith Sharp still hadn't called, and we began to suspect there was a problem. The next morning, Tom and I were eating breakfast in the hotel when a huge and somewhat frightening-looking guy came into the restaurant and hulked toward us. He sported long, unkempt hair, dirty sweatpants, and the gap-toothed smile of a road agent in a spaghetti western. He thrust out his hand. "Nice to meet you, boys. I'm Keith Sharp."

Keith sat down, ordered a coffee, and apologized in his thick Staffordshire accent for missing us at the airport. He said he had been coming to pick us up when the Cessna "blew an engine." When people say an engine "blew," they usually mean that it made a funny rattling noise and refused to start. But in this case, Keith assured us, the engine had actually "blown," i.e., expired with an explosive bang. Metal fragments had flown in every direction. Oil had sprayed all over the windshield. The pilot, an excitable Chilean, had begun babbling in fear. "Just shut up and put it down there," Keith had ordered, pointing to a pond the size of a hockey rink among the hills of bare granite. The pilot had managed to make a dead stick landing, and Keith had radioed the Coast Guard to come and pick them up in a helicopter. If the pond hadn't been there, Keith said, they almost certainly would have been killed. But he was only telling the story by way of apology. After all, it had happened yesterday— ancient history, in this neck of the woods. In the Arctic, you can't go around talking about the bad stuff that happened yesterday or you'll never get around to the bad stuff that happened this morning.

Now the plane was stranded fifty miles west of here. It wouldn't be going anywhere until mechanics arrived, flew into the lake with a new engine, and installed it on the spot. "That was the plane we were going to use today," Keith said. "So you're lucky you weren't in it." He said it would probably cost eighty thousand dollars to put the plane back in the air again.

Farther south, floatplanes are as common as taxi cabs. But Rankin Inlet is pretty much the ragged edge of civilization, and there wasn't another float-equipped airplane in town. This meant we wouldn't be visiting the Barrens anytime soon. "Living in the North teaches you the virtues of patience," Keith explained. "What you do most of the time is wait. You wait for the airplane. You wait on the weather. You wait and wait and wait, and while you wait, you hemorrhage money." Paying for our bacon-and-egg specials, at sixteen dollars each, I began to appreciate his point.

We climbed into Keith's pickup truck and went for a drive. The road continued for a few miles, then petered out at the edge of the Barrens. Tom got out to stalk a ground squirrel. As we sat in the truck watching, he knelt down and shot the squirrel with a big telephoto lens. The ground squirrel wasn't a bull caribou, but at least it was a wild animal. "We might see a rabbit," Keith said hopefully, peering out the window as we drove slowly back into town.

Keith told us he'd spent a lot of his childhood reading escape novels like *Robinson Crusoe*. He always wanted to see the wilderness, and he got his first chance in 1967, when he came to Canada at the age of twenty-eight. He fell in love with the country and worked all over western Canada in construction, building dams and bridges. He specialized in difficult concrete work. "Anytime you're driving along and you see a structure with curved concrete, that's me."

When Keith arrived in Rankin in 1971, he found lots of construction work. He met a young Inuit woman named Alma, and they became an item. It was a little rough at first, he said, getting accepted by the locals. "I was sleeping with an Eskimo girl, and that was a no-no in those days."

One building inspector in particular didn't like him. "He called me on the phone one night and started berating me. He said, 'You're a slimy Limey,' and so forth. I didn't really take offence because he was drunk. Then he said, 'You know what? You don't work for Baert Construction. You work for Fart Construction.'

"Calling my employer Fart Construction, well . . . that was going too far. I went down to the pub and walked in, took off his glasses, and knocked out six of his teeth. He called the police and charged me with assault. I happened to be friends with the local RCMP officer, so he went easy on me. But I couldn't get any construction work after that. I lived in a shack with Alma and trapped and fished for a couple of years. I loved being out on the land. The size of the country and its silence got inside me. I could never live in a city again."

A while later we arrived at Keith's place, a big wooden house with no windows. He said that when you woke up, you couldn't tell whether it was day or night. "Ingenious idea, don't you think? I designed it."

He introduced us to Alma and to a couple of his daughters, and told us the names of the fat little grandchildren toddling around on the floor. He fired up the stove to prepare us a lunch of his special recipe, "Caribou a la Sharp," which evidently consists of tossing a freshly thawed bleeding hunk of caribou haunch into a red-hot frying pan. "Sometimes I'll throw some curry powder in there," he explained. "People tell me I'm quite a cook." After the hunk of meat had sizzled for

79

five minutes, he sawed off some large pieces and tossed them on our plates. The presentation was a little basic, but the meat was delicious, sweet as spring lamb and tender enough to be cut with a spoon. To feed his large family, Keith shoots about fifteen caribou a year.

Keith's kitchen is apparently like one of those legendary restaurants in New York or San Francisco—sooner or later, everyone who visits Nunavut passes through here. "Pierre Trudeau sat right there," Keith remarked, pointing at my chair with a blood-smeared knife. "Very quiet, courteous man. He came here with his boys to see the land."

He said General Norman Schwarzkopf ("a bona fide redneck") and General Colin Powell ("a real gentleman") had also eaten lunch here, en route to one of Keith's outpost camps. During his twenty-odd years in the tourist business, he's had guests from all over the world. He told us people from Chicago are cranky. Germans are obedient, and people from Minneapolis "wouldn't say boo to a goose."

Keith was the mayor of Rankin in 1995, and he has done almost everything you can do in the North. "I've built houses, hauled freight. I've made and lost a million dollars several times over. But the money comes and goes. One day you're in the chips, next day you're broke. Everything is so bloody expensive up here, and as a territory, we have no idea where we're going. We've got this new political entity, Nunavut, and everyone is all excited about it. But be realistic, how are we going to support ourselves? Tourism? There's no bloody tourists. The average tourist is too much of a sissy to come here."

While we waited for the aircraft mechanics to arrive, Tom and I stayed at Keith's house. It was hard to tell how many people comprised his extended family. The television played twenty-four hours a day, and when I got up to pee in the middle of the night, kids would be lying all over the living room, on the sofa and on the floor. I'd pick my way through the tangled bodies while in the corner Colonel Klink clenched his hands furiously and cursed Hogan's latest antics. Every morning, Tom and I would walk down to the hotel and have breakfast.

Finally two weary-looking mechanics, both named Bob, flew in from Thompson. They took a helicopter out to the pond where the airplane was sitting and got to work. Later on, they told us they'd stayed in a soggy tent with a .243 rifle, a rubber mattress, and a moldy haunch of caribou meat. Replacing the engine wasn't exactly a straightforward job. The new Continental engine weighed six hundred pounds, and they had no way to lift it onto the nose of the airplane. They didn't have a block and tackle, and even if they had, there was nothing to hang it from. The nearest tree was five hundred miles away.

Bob and Bob used their brains and by some miracle lifted the new engine into place, got it running, taxied the plane back and forth a few times to test it, then said a little prayer, poured on the coal, and took off for Rankin Inlet. Keith was glad to have the Cessna back in operation, but the plane didn't have a proper oil gauge for the new motor. Under the law, that meant city slickers like us couldn't travel in it. Keith and the two Bobs could, presumably because their lives weren't as valuable. Bob and Bob ordered an oil gauge from the factory in Wichita, assuring us that as soon as it arrived, we were cleared for takeoff. Every night in the coffee shop, they gave us an update on the gauge's epic journey from Kansas to Nunavut. "It's like Keith told you," Bob said. "When you live in the North, you have to be good at waiting."

Tom and I waited, killing time. One day we went to a char fishing camp north of town and spent the afternoon chatting with the Inuit people and eating blubber. They kept a dog tied up to a post about a hundred yards from camp. If the dog started barking in the middle of the night, they knew a bear was coming. An old man told us you have to pick the right sort of dog to act as a sentinel. It has to be a good barker, and it can't be too shy or it will cringe and lie down when it sees a bear. He himself had been attacked by polar bears three times, and he had big scars across his head to prove it. "There are good bears and bad bears, happy bears and bad-tempered bears. They're no different than dogs or people."

Another day Keith invited us to a wedding. The ceremony took place inside a group of linked-up double-wide trailers called the Church of the Holy Comforter. As the crowd gathered, pretty bridesmaids roared up on ATVs, wearing high heels and the traditional hooded parkas called *motiqs*. The groom was wearing a big pressure bandage on his arm. Keith, who speaks fluent Inuktitut, albeit with a Staffordshire accent, talked to the groom and told us what had happened. "He went whale-hunting yesterday. When he threw a harpoon at a beluga, the whale threw it back at him."

The groom's arm injury prompted some of the young bridesmaids to whisper and giggle among themselves. "They're speculating about whether he'll be up to his matrimonial chores this evening," Keith explained. As we trooped into the church, a gang of little kids sprinted around the mud parking lot in the cold sun, blowing bubbles.

The next day, the precious oil gauge arrived. The Bobs reacted with incredulous disgust when they took it out of the box. It was the wrong gauge. "Why doesn't this surprise me?" one Bob asked.

Keith didn't seem much upset. He's been living in the North for so long that he's immune to being pissed off. "I've

82

had four heart attacks," he said. "Now I try to see it all as a comedy."

Keith said that a local drilling company owed him some time on their helicopter, and he was going to ask them for it. The helicopter was based at a drilling camp about a hundred miles west of Rankin Inlet. Light helicopters lease out for about a thousand dollars an hour, so it made sense for us to go to the helicopter rather than have it come to us. The next morning, we hitched a ride on a wheel-equipped Cessna that was heading to the drilling camp. Keith's twenty-year-old son George came along with us. Tom and I hadn't brought groceries, because Keith overruled it. "We'll live off the land," he said. "You don't have to buy food around here. It's a waste of money."

We climbed into the helicopter when we arrived at the drilling camp, and at last, yes, we were flying into the Barrens! As we cruised over cinematic-looking waterfalls and decorative ponds, it was hard not to think that we were flying over some computer-generated landscape at Universal Studios. At the Kazan, we flared in for a landing next to Keith's outpost camp, a plywood shack perched on a low rise above the river. The pilot left the engine running, and we hurriedly climbed out. A group of American doctors were waiting for us. They'd been stranded here for days, thanks to the blown engine on the Cessna. With their sooty faces, whiskered chins and slightly crazed eyes they looked like characters from the movie *Deliverance*. "Saw hundreds of caribou every day!" one of them screamed happily over the roar of the helicopter. "We ran out of food, but we ate fish. Bobby strangled a ptarmigan with his bare hands!"

The doctors climbed aboard, and the helicopter roared away. We picked up our bags and headed downhill to the cabin. Next to it was a yellow Bombardier half-track with a smashed windshield. "A grizzly broke into it in the spring and drank a gallon of anti-freeze," Keith explained. "Must have died a horrible death, poor bugger."

Keith led us into the shack, dropped his bags on the floor and pointed to a rusty 12-gauge shotgun leaning against the wall. "Do you know how to use that gun? It's fully loaded in case of a bear emergency. Man, it's good to be here. Anyone want coffee?"

We picked bunk beds and started unpacking. Keith glanced out the door and muttered to his son. "George, go and shoot that caribou."

Tom and I looked outside. A magnificent bull caribou was standing on the edge of the river, about a hundred yards away. Water slathered down from its muzzle as it lifted its head from the river. It looked like the caribou on the Canadian twenty-five-cent piece. Tom grabbed his camera. George opened a gun case and took out a scope-sighted rifle. The gun, a sleek Remington, belonged to his sister Sylvia. We'd met Sylvia a few days before. She was a no-nonsense young woman with short hair and camouflage army pants. She told us she liked hunting muskox. She said muskox will charge anything shorter than they are, so you have to stand tall when you're near the herd. "I drive up to them on the snowmobile and stand on the seat."

"How close can you get?"

"About ten feet."

"So then what do you do?"

"Pick the one I want and shoot it in the head."

Sylvia was recently single, due to the fact that her husband, a construction worker from Quebec, had been murdered by his girlfriend. Sylvia wasn't the type to cry over spilled milk, and she told us she planned to support herself by becoming an RCMP officer. As George searched his bag for ammunition, we all watched the caribou from the doorway. Tom braced his telephoto against the door frame and shot dozens of exposures. Would the bull finish drinking and amble away in time? Or would George get the gun loaded and cancel the caribou's ticket? I tried not to take sides. It was like watching a golfer coping with a three-million-dollar putt at Augusta.

George was silent as he rummaged through his bag. He had said only about five words since we met him. He was a reclusive sort who'd spent most of the trip out here reading a hardback copy of *Angela's Ashes*. He read with excruciating slowness, moving his lips and holding a small plastic ruler against the page. He told me it was the second copy of the book he'd purchased. He'd allowed someone to look at the first one, but they "bent one of the pages," so he bought another. I hoped that Frank McCourt appreciated having such an avid reader up here.

George was still looking for shells when Keith abruptly changed his mind. He closed the door and went back to his coffee. "Forget about it, George. It's too far away anyway."

The bull caribou walked away, never knowing how close it had come to being in a frying pan with Keith's curry sprinkled all over its buttocks. "We'll just wait," Keith said. "We'll be seeing them a lot closer than that." Sure enough, a few minutes later, a group of caribou walked right past the front door. Before Keith could order the hit, Tom seized his camera and we slipped out the door.

The four caribou grazed like Shetland ponies in the front yard for a few minutes, then wandered down toward the river. As they browsed among some riverbank willows, Tom and I stalked them, crawling on hands and knees, keeping the wind

85

in our favor. When we were about twenty-five steps away, the cow of the group raised her head and looked at us with complete boredom, as if to say, "May I help you?"

The Kazan River is one of three major waterways that drain eastward across the Barrens. Keith's outpost cabin is situated right between the calving grounds of the Kaminuriak and the Beverly caribou herds. The animals are occasionally preyed upon by wolves, grizzlies, and human beings, but they display little fear of humans. Cows and calves can outrun a wolf. The bulls, burdened with extra body weight and hefty antlers, are more wary. Over the next few days, we spotted an occasional grand bull bedded alone on a hillside. We tried stalking close a number of times, but the caribou always sensed our presence and moved off.

After Tom and I got over our initial concern about our lack of groceries, we saw that indeed, there was food all around. The so-called Barren Lands are actually an enormous groceteria, with the principal ground cover consisting of dense, shin-high brush so laden with berries that you can't kneel down without staining your pants. The hillsides are alive with caribou, hares, and ptarmigan, and the rivers are full of fish. At mealtime every evening, Keith would smack his hands together, glance at me, and announce, "Right then, go fetch me a nice trout of, I'd say, about eight or nine pounds, will you?"

"Yes sir."

Rigging up my fly rod, I'd head down to the river, wade into the water in my rubber boots, and cast a steamer fly. It hadn't been difficult to fulfill my goal of catching a large trout. In fact, the fishing was so easy that I felt it was rude to bother the trout for more than an hour or two every day. I'd cast, retrieve the fly with a vigorous stripping action, and before it got halfway in there would be a wild swirl and a violent strike. Aided by the current, a large trout would easily peel off a hundred yards of line. Tom would take pictures as I staggered around in the water, trying to subdue the fish. The problem wasn't catching a trout; it was catching one small enough to fit on the barbecue. Some of them were fifteen to twenty pounds, much too large for Keith's preferences. If the hook was deep inside their jaws, I'd have to haul them up onto the bank and use forceps to remove it. The cold, oxygenated water seemed to make the fish incredibly energetic, and as I tried to immobilize them they thrashed and bounced furiously. Tom, who has shot crimes, weddings, and wars, said I reminded him of a cop wrestling with a skinny biker on angel dust. After capturing and releasing three or four trout, I'd finally get one to suit Keith's specifications. Braining it with a rock, I'd haul it up to the cabin and walk in the door spattered with water, blood, and muck. "Did you order an eight-pound trout, sir?"

After a couple of days of exploring, Tom still hadn't gotten close enough for a money shot of a bull caribou. So Keith gassed up a boat and took us down the river. The Kazan is a canoeist's dream. It's broad and smooth and flows with latent power through a wide valley of gentle, green hills. On a warm day, you could drowse with the paddle across your knees, the sun on your shoulders, and still average five miles an hour. You wouldn't want to sleep too soundly, though. A few miles downstream of camp, Keith shut off the motor and we drifted. Ahead, we could hear the white noise of rapids.

Keith beached the boat and insisted that we sit and wait while he checked the shore for Akthuk, the grizzly, which apparently favors these rapids as a fishing hole. "They leave fish carcasses as a calling card," he said. "A grizzly cleans a fish so nicely you'd think it was done by a man with a knife."

Keith disappeared for ten minutes, then returned, satisfied that we had the rapids to ourselves. We walked smooth rocks worn into fabulous shapes by the age-old rasping of water and ice. The sun was warm, and the breeze was vigorous enough to keep the blackflies away. We sat on the humps of worn granite, satisfied to laze awhile. Keith was reclining on his side, eyeing the landscape like a grizzly bear with his beard wafting in the breeze. "Keep your camera ready, Tom," he said. "Last year ten thousand of them came here and stayed for about four days. Place smelled like a barnyard. You could have sat on that rock and taken pictures all day. They were swimming the river and climbing out right there, water pouring off them. Magnificent sight."

"Do you think they'll be back this year?"

"Maybe," said Keith, with a shrug. "This is the North. Who knows?"

The next day, Keith called Alma on the VHF radio and learned that Bob and Bob had received the proper oil gauge for the Cessna. The plane was now legally equipped for flying passengers. Keith told her to send it to pick us up.

We waited all day, but no plane. We wondered if the engine had failed again. That night, Keith tried to raise Alma on the radio, but he couldn't get through. The radio sounded like a blender full of nails. "Probably sunspots," Keith grunted. "We could be cut off for days."

It started to rain. George curled up in his bunk with *Angela's Ashes*. Keith boiled up a pail of instant coffee on the Coleman stove. We kept our bags stacked outside, in the lee of the cabin. I relaxed in my saggy bunk, reading an old Isaac Asimov paperback with a couple of chapters missing. Rain needled the roof. The silence in the cabin was interrupted only by Keith's snoring and an occasional fart. I kept listen-

88

ing for the sound of a distant engine while pretending not to care whether I heard one or not. I felt like I was doing field research for an advanced class in Zen waiting.

Finally, late in the day, from across the river, came the throbbing of rotors. It was not a plane but a helicopter. We hurried outside. It was like seeing the air cavalry coming. The chopper was pure white and shone like a tern against the stormy sky. Flaring in over the tundra, it landed in a roar of whipping vegetation. We ran toward it, hauling bags and gear. The pilot climbed out and left the engine running. "Hey, Tom," I shouted. "Do you mind if I ride up front?"

"Go for it."

I handed the pilot my rucksack. "Should I get in?"

"Yeah, go ahead."

AS IT TURNS OUT, nobody dies.

The helicopter is shimmying and beginning to lift off when the door tears open and the pilot leaps across my lap, seizing the control stick. For a long period of four or five seconds, the helicopter trembles and dances like a stallion. Then the engine RPMs begin to subside and the danger passes.

Without so much as a comment, the pilot climbs into the cockpit and straps himself in. My three companions, looking a bit spooked, also climb in and fasten their seat belts. We proceed with a normal takeoff. Nobody says a word. I consider apologizing to the pilot. But occasionally one commits an error so extreme you can't just say, "Sorry about that, mate."

We fly in silence for twenty minutes, with the hilly, stagy-looking tundra rolling past beneath us. The pilot, a tired-faced veteran who looks as if he already had been having a bad day, stares straight ahead. Finally, we land on a mud airstrip at

89

a mining camp at Ferguson Lake, where we plan to transfer to a Cessna. The pilot maintains a stony silence, declining to move as we all climb out.

When the chopper is empty, I give the pilot a sporty wave, then close the door, which on an A-Star is not that complicated an affair. You close it, and it makes an authoritative click. It's a door; you get the idea. Given my previous screw-up, I nevertheless use a bit more emphasis than normal to close it. I test the door once or twice, then heft my bags and scurry away with my head lowered to avoid decapitation. Standing well off to one side, I lay my bags on the ground and watch the helicopter do its hell-raising takeoff.

When the helicopter is about a hundred yards in the air, the door blows open. Driven by rotor blast, the door swings violently back and forth. I can see the pilot's arm as he tries to grab it. Each time he clutches at the door handle the helicopter slews wildly and the door flits out of his grasp.

Finally he captures the door and pulls it shut. The helicopter speeds away, and my buddy Tom cocks an eyebrow. "You sure gave him something to talk about at dinner tonight."

"It's his own fault," I say. "He was too trusting."

We board the wheel-equipped Cessna Caravan and carry on. It's raining, and we have to fly low. We're supposed to be back in Rankin Inlet before nightfall, but I'm not betting on it.

|||||||||||||||||||||||||||||||||||||||||||||||||||||

Bonefish

DUNDEE

◇◇◇◇◇

*G*etting serious about fishing is like enrolling in an MA program. A certain amount of field work is expected. You're agreeing to buy expensive airplane tickets and go fishing in places you can't afford. You're signing on to willingly spend many days pursuing species like steelhead, muskellunge, Atlantic salmon, and bonefish, all of which are notoriously difficult to catch. While pursuing these contrary species, you're expected to study at the elbow of recognized old masters, who will treat you with the kind of disdain that school headmasters used to reserve for nitwits in a new class of freshmen.

Part of being a serious angler is learning to use the fly rod. My mother bought me my first fly rod on my fortieth birthday, and I spent a lot of time learning how to use it. I read some articles about fly-fishing for bass, pike and other species that lived in my neighborhood, but although I caught a nice pike now and then, it seemed to me that fly-fishing didn't work as well as other techniques. I wasn't learning to fly-fish in order to catch fewer fish. I was already good at that. If reducing one's effectiveness is equivalent to being more sporting, why not just fish with no lure or, for that matter, with no line? Better yet, why not just pour yourself a double and try to catch a rainbow trout in the kitchen sink? Wouldn't that be the most challenging undertaking of all?

A few years after my fortieth birthday, I had gone on a midwinter trip to the Bahamas with my buddy Paul Quarrington. We had fished in the open sea in a big boat and in the shallows in a small boat with the legendary local guide, Ansil Saunders. As I mentioned earlier, we even caught some bonefish, with spinning rods and small hooks baited with prawns. The bonefish scoffed up our baits with gusto and fought spiritedly on our light rods. It had been a new experience for both of us and a noteworthy development in our fishing careers. But there was one small problem. To catch a bonefish on a spinning rod, you drift around in the shallows until you see a school, then toss the bait toward them. They swim over and gobble it up. After P.Q. and I had caught about a dozen bonefish, I understood why most anglers eschew the use of bait. It's too easy. If you handicapped yourself with an artificial fly, I thought, bonefish just might be the perfect challenge. In the bar on our last night, as we reviewed the day's performance, Paul expressed the same opinion. "Now that we've put a few bonefish under our belts on conventional tackle, we should come back and try them with fly rods."

"I agree, Thresher."

Over the years, Paul and I have come to address each other by nicknames. He sometimes calls me Mako and I sometimes call him Thresher. Our girlfriends would have no idea who we're talking about. Nicknames don't really make much sense; everyone calls a friend of mine "Nicky," but nobody knows how he acquired the name.

At the end of the bar, a weather-beaten American yachtsman sat drinking rum with his girlfriend, a nut-brown blonde half his age. You can walk into any bar in the Caribbean and see this same couple. I addressed the man. "Which island in the Bahamas has the most bonefish?"

"Bonefish?" he said. "I don't think it matters where you go. They're all over the place."

"I'm guessing you've traveled a lot in the Bahamas."

He smiled. "You guess right."

"In your opinion, what's the nicest island?"

He thought about it for a moment, took a deliberative sip of rum. His girlfriend turned toward him and murmured something. He took another sip and sighed heavily, as if the question bothered him. "I don't know. I guess you'd have to say Elbow Cay is pretty damn near perfect."

Paul and I clinked glasses. Next time we'd go to Elbow Cay. And we'd take fly rods.

It would be worthwhile at this point to examine the mechanics and underlying raison d'être of the fly rod. Some fish eat minnows and baitfish. Others eat insects and invertebrates, and these species are attracted to artificial flies. Despite what many fly-fishing snobs imply, the fly, constructed of tiny wisps of feather, deer hair, and so on, is not aesthetically superior to other types of artificial bait. It's simply the only lure that attracts the fish that eat bugs. Flies weigh next to nothing, and they are impossible to cast with conventional equipment. Thus the invention of the fly rod.

Back in the 1600s, when Charles I was running England into the ground and John Donne was the vicar of St. Dunstan

parish, Donne's friend Izaak Walton was stalking the banks
of the nearby river Lea in search of trout and grayling, using
a twelve-foot tapered rod and a line made from woven horse-
hair. (He believed the tail hairs from a black horse worked
best.) Walton's line had a butt section built from nine horse-
hairs braided together, and it tapered down to a fine leader of
only two hairs, which would have had a breaking strength of
about two to three pounds. With the line drooping from the
end of his homemade wooden pole, Walton would "cast" the
fly as best he could and drift it past likely eddies and holding areas. He must have been very skilled, because he would
often subdue four-pound trout with this flimsy rig. Catching a fish heavier than the breaking strength of one's line is
one good way of separating the men from the boys. Walton
in fact once commented that "he that cannot kill a trout of
twenty inches long with two hairs does not deserve the name
of angler."

In the early 1700s, British army officers began experimenting with bamboo rods in India, fishing for the elusive
mahseer in the foothills of the Himalayas. They returned
to Blighty with bundles of bamboo, and English rod makers
began building the first split-cane fly rods. The fly rod takes
the principle of casting and turns it upside down. With a conventional fishing rod, the angler flings the lure and its weight
pulls line off the reel. With a fly rod, the lure weighs nothing,
so the angler casts the line instead. Bamboo fly rods were
stiff enough to allow the angler to whip a silk fly line back
and forth, building up enough speed that the line itself would
loop out across the stream, carrying the fly with it.

Casting a fly line is equivalent to swinging a golf club, in
the sense that few people can do it with the sort of power,
grace, and confidence that make witnesses involuntarily gasp

and whisper "Wow." When I got back home from Bimini, I rolled up my sleeves and began practicing. I practiced on the lawn, and I practiced on the water. I practiced enough that I could hit a small target at forty-five feet. I assumed that casting a fly rod was like riding a bicycle; after you reached a certain level of proficiency, it was always there. I found out later that this was incorrect. Some skills require constant maintenance. Landing airplanes on aircraft carriers is apparently so tricky that pilots who take only a week or two off have to take brush-up lessons when they return. Casting a fly rod may not be quite as dangerous. But if you think you can leave your fly rod on the rack for an entire winter, then pick it up and hit a bonefish-sized target at forty-five feet on your first cast, you're liable to end up with a Number 6 Gotcha affixed to your ear as a small lesson in humility.

Thresher and I learned this when we sallied forth to Elbow Cay. Time goes quickly if you count off your life by fishing trips. It had been two years since our trip to Bimini. We caught a taxi to the airport, driving through the slop and pallor of a cold February morning in Toronto, got airborne, had breakfast, and watched the earth below us turn from white to brown to Kentucky green. When we landed in Miami at noon, it was ninety-two in the shade. We didn't really have to go all the way to the Bahamas to pursue bonefish with our fly rods. If you head south from Miami on A1A, you can be bombing through the Keys within an hour, and every tidal flat along the way holds bonefish. Key Largo and Big Pine Key are choked with fishing lodges, guide services, and Jimmy Buffett–style beer joints built on creosote timbers above the water. But we were on our way to the big leagues, so we retrieved our luggage, boarded a small American Eagle turbo-prop, and carried on.

The little Saab droned eastward across the Atlantic. Soon the deep blue waters of the open sea gave way to the Bahamas, golden islets of sand, and jade-green tidal shallows. Somewhere down in those invisible shallows was our legendary prey—the bonefish. This trip was supposed to be a vacation, but as our plane cruised over those tidal flats, I felt a little like we were headed for graduate school.

When our airplane landed on the island of Great Abaco, we went through customs, claimed our bags, and hailed a cab for the ride to the ferry terminal. A big hurricane named Floyd had rampaged across Abaco the previous winter, and the signs of damage were still evident—sunken boats, damaged buildings and palm trees that looked like frazzled hockey sticks. But the Bahamians are a hard-working, good-natured people, and adversity is nothing new to them. "I spent the hurricane crouched in a concrete cistern," laughed our cab driver, a fat black lady with a huge straw hat on her head. "It was very bad, sir. Very bad. But we will rebuild, just like we always do."

At the north end of Abaco we caught the ferry to Elbow Cay, the last barrier island separating the Bahamas from the open Atlantic. The ferry took us on a twenty-minute ride to Hope Town, a small English-style fishing village with narrow streets and tiny, pastel-painted cottages. We'd booked a guide ahead of time, a veteran of repute named Bonefish Dundee, and he met us at the wharf. I'd expected a black guy, a native Bahamian. But Bonefish Dundee was wiry and white, about fifty years old, with aviator sunglasses, a dangling cigarette, and a tough-guy accent that sounded Australian. He looked like Paul Hogan, the star of Crocodile Dundee. Our guide said his accent was Bahamian, though, and that his family had come to the Bahamas many generations ago, as United Empire Loyalists.

"My real name is Maitland Lowe," he growled. "But everyone calls me Bonefish Dundee. It wasn't my idea. But everyone kept calling me that, so I quit fighting it."

We climbed into Maitland's van and bounced down a long dusty road to the Abaco Inn, a group of small cottages overlooking a deserted beach. The manager assigned us a cabin and explained that we wouldn't need a key, because even though the island has five thousand residents—many of whom are descended from American slaves—there's virtually no crime. "In twenty-seven years we've never had a case of theft," she said. "The island doesn't even have a police officer."

By now it was late in the afternoon. So we unpacked and then went straight to the restaurant, where we shoveled some delicious hot slabs of grilled grouper. After dinner, we retired to the open-air bar, where we did our best to deplete the bartender's supply of Caribbean rum. It was an exciting prospect to be stalking bonefish for the first time with our fly rods, so as we stumbled back to our cabin we were full of great expectations. We were full of rum, too. P.Q. was so gassed that he promptly fell asleep on the couch, fully dressed. An hour later he got up to pee and gave the wall in the bathroom a good splattering. Then he tried to climb into my bed, although he later made me swear not to mention that part.

The next morning, after gobbling a few aspirins and swearing off rum for the rest of our lives, we walked gingerly down to the main lodge for a bite of breakfast. As we picked at our eggs, Maitland showed up, with his sunglasses on and a cigarette dangling from the side of his mouth. "Well, sirs . . . do you want to sit on your asses the whole bloody morning or do you want to go fishing?"

One of the things you notice, when you fish with a guide of some accomplishment, is that he treats you like a peon. We

forced down our eggs, gathered our tackle, and joined Maitland at his skiff. Minutes later, we were sledding down Abaco
Sound. Everywhere in the Bahamas, it seems, the water is
only a few yards deep. Underlain by golden sand, mottled
coral and turtle grass, the sea takes on the same colour as
a 7-Up bottle. As we sped along, the shallow bottom flashed
beneath us, and small barracudas and rays darted away from
the boat's flying shadow. When Maitland finally slowed down,
the sun felt like a heat lamp on our bare heads. "Put on your
hats, boys," he said. "It's going to be quiet today. Good conditions for fly-rodding."

You can't work two fly rods from one boat, so P.Q. and
I flipped a coin. I won the toss. I climbed up onto the casting platform and went over the checklist that I'd memorized
over the last few days. Okay, shake out fifteen feet of line.
Hold your fly in your rod hand. Strip off another fifteen or
twenty feet and hold the coils loosely in your free hand. Now
you're loaded, ready to shoot a cast at the first bonefish you
see. Take a quick survey of the deck to make sure that there
are no cleats or loose ropes to snag your line. Are you balanced comfortably on the balls of your feet? Are your knees
slightly flexed? Look now, look . . . you're standing on the line,
you idiot!

While I conducted this tense conversation with myself,
Maitland unlimbered his sixteen-foot push pole. The tide was
coming in, and the tidal flat was flooding with water. Maitland
climbed up onto the platform, leaned on the pole. We glided
forward. Our voices dropped to a whisper as we scanned the
water around us. With each wisp of cloud moving across the
sun, the water changed from green to turquoise to blue, and
then to green again. An occasional puff of silt erupted as a
sting ray fled from our shadow. Farther away, a school of small

jacks crossed our path. I consider myself to be a half-decent spotter of wildlife, but I was no match for Maitland. When I pointed to a far-off flash of movement, he wouldn't even turn his head. "That's only a barracuda, sir," he'd say, having spotted it himself quite a while earlier. Generally, we kept silent, and with each passing minute, the tension rose higher. There was a palpable sense that we'd see a bonefish anytime now. But would the fish see us first?

Finally a trio of bonefish came nosing along the bottom, headed our way. Maitland immobilized the boat by driving his pole into the sand. Heart thudding, I made ready for the cast. My first attempt fell short, so I raised the rod for another. But in my haste, the line ripped the water and the bonefish streaked away. "Don't yank your line off the water like that," Maitland grumbled. "If you blow your first cast, strip it in gently, then try again."

After a few minutes, another trio of bonefish came along. This time, my cast skidded sideways in the breeze and slapped the water about twenty feet off target. I tried again, and a loop of line caught itself around the butt of the rod.

Maitland was terse. "Very large bonefish right in front of you, sir. Cast quickly now, before he sees the boat."

The loner was coming toward us, sniffing the bottom. I was madly trying to untangle my line. He was big, all right; even from this distance he looked like a chunk of stove wood. I was already rattled, and the size of the fish didn't help. "Buck fever" is a term that's usually associated with hunting, but it can happen anytime you see a quarry better than you deserve. 99 Rushing my cast, I snapped the line into a forward roll and caught the hook on something behind me. I turned around to see that it was snagged in Maitland's wrist.

"Oh brother," I said. "Sorry about that."

He plucked the hook out. "Don't be sorry about that," he retorted. "Be sorry that you missed that bloody fish."

This was a disgrace. I stepped down off the platform and handed Paul the rod. "Your turn, partner."

My buck fever seemed contagious, because Paul's casting was no better than mine. Maitland maneuvered us over to the mouth of a huge flat, where schools of bonefish were cruising past like Manhattan taxicabs at rush hour. Paul slapped the water to the left and right. Each time he shot a cast, the water erupted with the tails of stampeding fish. At one point, Maitland hissed in warning as a school of easily a hundred bonefish came cruising right toward us. It was my turn again. A dozen-odd fish passed us broadside, so close that a nine-year-old kid with a Pocket Fisherman could have hit any one of them. Maddeningly, I couldn't seem to make the line work. Instead of uncoiling in graceful arcs, the fly line writhed back and forth overhead in wild snaps and dropped onto the water like a decapitated snake. My game was in total collapse.

Strangely, though, one of the fish swam over and scoffed down the fly. I reared back on the rod and set the hook. This particular bonefish must have had a learning disability, because instead of taking on a blistering run, it swam around in confused circles. I applied pressure with the rod until the fish suddenly got frightened and took off. P.Q. and Maitland cheered. The reel screamed as the bonefish sped across the flat. My ninety-foot line was attached to two hundred yards of Dacron backing attached with a nail knot. A week ago, the know-it-all clerk at the expensive fly-fishing store in Toronto had insisted on tying the knot for me. "You better let me do that," he said. "If you're going all the way to the Bahamas, you don't want to lose a nice fish because of a knot failure."

As soon as tension hit the backing, his expertly tied knot

fell apart. Maitland leaped out of the boat, and galloped through the shin-deep water. Fifty feet from the boat, he seized the fly line and tried to hand-line the fish, but it was gone. He walked back to the boat and demanded to know who'd tied the knot.

I didn't know which was worse, saying I'd tied it myself or admitting that I'd let someone else do it. So I told him the truth. He issued a choked laugh, as if he couldn't believe any of this. I couldn't believe it either. Was this a nightmare? Would I hear the clock radio beeping in a few minutes and realize this was my own private version of *Groundhog Day*?

Maitland climbed into the boat, adjusted his baseball cap to a philosophical angle, and lit a cigarette. He looked relieved, as if he'd finally realized that this whole undertaking was supposed to be a comedy. Taking a puff, he fired up the motor. "That's all for today," he said.

We looked at our watches. We'd only been out for a few hours.

"The tide is going out," he said. "The bones will head out to deeper water and won't be back until this evening."

Paul and I were crestfallen. Had we blown our one chance?

Back at the pier, Maitland dropped us off and gave us both a thumbs-up, as if to say, *Don't worry, fellows, I won't tell anyone.*

That night, as we sat in the bar, P.Q. and I got down to some serious deliberation. On the way in, Maitland had told us that he was booked solid for the next couple of days, which is guide language for "I'm washing my hair." The bartender told us there were no other guides on the island. Whatever social conditions had driven the criminals off had apparently eliminated the fishing guides, too. It was a beautiful night, crickets singing and palm leaves rattling in the breeze, but we couldn't relax, knowing our fishing trip was turning into a rout. "Well, Thresher," I finally said, slamming my glass down on the bartop. "I guess I'll have to come out of retirement."

"I beg your pardon?"

"I used to be a fishing guide, when I was a young feller. Remember? What's so complicated about catching bonefish? We'll rent a boat, get some maps, and go find some fish ourselves."

Paul didn't look too excited by my solution, but what choice did we have?

The next morning we found a local marina operator who was reckless enough to rent us a boat, a seventeen-foot Boston Whaler. After listening to a long and confusing lecture about flare pistols, VHF emergency channels, etc. etc. (this being the ocean, after all), we fired up the motor and headed for a place that looked like surefire fish habitat. At least it did on the hydrographic charts. "It's called Snake Cay," I said.

"We're not fishing for snakes."

"Look at this great bottom structure," I said, tapping my finger on the map as we cruised across Abaco Sound. "Up in Canada, it would be an excellent walleye spot."

"We're not fishing for walleyes."

"Fish are fish," I said. I gestured toward the steering wheel. "Maybe you'd like to be the guide?"

When we reached Snake Cay, it looked like a mudfield after a heavy rain. Paul scanned the flat. "Mako, there's no water."

"That's okay, the tide is coming in."

"When?"

"I have no idea."

We sat in the boat for the better part of an hour, baking in the sun, until water, ever so slowly, began trickling onto the flat. As the water rose, we followed it. We soon found out that our heavy Boston Whaler, lovely boat that it is, drew a lot more water than a bonefish skiff. Our boat plowed the bottom in a foot of water. Maitland's skiff drew four inches. It was apparent that we had to get out and push.

It was hot, sweaty work, but I didn't mind. We deserved to be punished, both of us, and what fitter punishment than pushing a thousand-pound skiff through stingray-infested water with the sun beating down on your head? We took turns, one playing the role of outboard motor while the other fished. For twenty minutes I pushed while Paul stood up on the casting deck, scanning the waters, seeing nothing. Then we switched, with the same results.

Finally I spotted a couple of dark shapes in the distance, and directed Paul to push us closer. When we were about forty feet away, it became apparent that the two large shapes were sharks, big black sharks about eight feet long. They were drifting in the shallows like submerged canoes. Paul, out of craven self-interest, decided to climb into the boat, depriving me of power.

We fished for two days like this, getting lots of exercise and drinking lots of water, but not seeing a single bonefish. That night we decided to give Maitland one more try. We rode bicycles to his house, a lemon-yellow, concrete monstrosity that once belonged to the folksinger Burl Ives. The house had been damaged by the hurricane, so Maitland and his twenty-five-year-old Cuban wife were fixing it up in exchange for free rent. We knocked on the door and asked him if he would take us fishing tomorrow. He thought about it for a few moments, lighting a cigarette and scowling at the ocean.

"Half a day?" we pleaded.

He went inside the house. We could hear him talking to his wife. They obviously weren't rich, and the standard rate for a guided bonefishing charter—$450 u.s. per day—is nothing to sneeze at. But this crime-free, cop-free island also seemed free of the normal work ethic. The way it usually works, you wave a couple of large bills in someone's face, and they scurry around and do your bidding. In Maitland's case, our offer of money only seemed to put him in a foul mood. At last he reappeared at the door. "I guess I could take you out tomorrow," he sighed. "But get your asses down to the beach and practice your casting."

That evening, instead of going to the calypso bar, Paul and I practiced with the fly rods. We were getting another chance, and we meant to make the best of it. So far, most of my experience with a fly rod had been with large, soggy pike flies, which add a couple of ounces of snappy weight to the leader. Bonefish flies add no weight at all, and I realized I had to unlearn my old reflexes and rebuild new ones.

Standing on the beach, Paul and I exchanged criticism of our techniques. After a full two hours of practice, we were shooting fifty-foot casts, and some were even fairly accurate. "Maitland can get the whole fly line airborne with one false cast," I said, whipping the rod a little harder.

Paul said, "You're not Maitland."

The next day we woke up clear-headed and keen. When Maitland cruised up to the wharf, we were waiting for him. We climbed into the boat and Maitland hit the throttle. He looked serious, clutching the wheel with that permanent cigarette jabbed in his mouth. Today was the real thing, no more screwing around.

For the better part of an hour we sped past reefs and islands and shallow rocky points. Eventually we arrived at a huge, utterly desolate tidal lagoon. In the narrow entrance to the lagoon, the tide boiled and swirled like a jungle river. As we trolled carefully through the rocky entrance, a pair of huge rays swam right under the boat. Maitland had no sooner deployed his push pole than we saw a large school of bonefish—about eighty of them, swimming along the beach with their backs out of the water. On Maitland's directions, Paul jumped out of the boat and stealthily began wading toward them. I got up on the casting platform in case we spotted some others.

Maitland pushed the boat in a different direction so that we wouldn't spoil Paul's stalk. We hadn't gone more than fifty feet when four large bonefish appeared out of nowhere, headed right toward us.

Reminding myself to let the line straighten out and load up the rod, I shot a perfect cast in their direction. The fly touched the water, settled. The largest fish approached the fly and sniffed it like a dog. I felt the faintest tug on the line (I'd rehearsed all this in my imagination a thousand times) and then I executed an approved Bonefish Dundee "strip strike," tugging on the line with a deft, apologetic jerk, then raising the rod tip in a sweeping strike. In response, the rod suddenly jumped to life. The reel exploded into a frenzied scream and Maitland issued a rebel yell. "You got him!"

That first run must have lasted a full minute, with the reel howling and the line racing out of the guides. Maitland kept shouting at me to hold the rod tip high. The rod was bent flat, but I muscled it high against the pressure. The line continued tearing off until I was down into the backing.

When the fish was perhaps two hundred yards across the lagoon, it made a right turn and sprinted the other way. Maitland warned me again to keep the rod high, so that the long line wouldn't snag on a coral outcrop.

"I love that sound, sir," Maitland declared, over the crazed whirring of the reel. "All this work, all these years of chasing bonefish—I do it just so that I can hear that sound."

A few moments later, a four-foot shark came quartering across the flat, probably attracted by the panicked vibrations of the bonefish. Maitland grabbed a gaffhook, jumped out of the boat and went rushing after it, swearing and waving the nasty hook as he galloped through the shallow water. The shark took off and Maitland returned, muttering curses at lemon sharks and all their relatives.

For the next fifteen minutes, under Maitland's fierce gaze, I kept the rod tip high and tried to avoid stupid mistakes. The fish was swimming in ever-smaller circles, and my arms were getting rubbery from the nonstop isometric pull of the rod.

It was twenty minutes on Maitland's wristwatch when the fish glided into his hands. I jumped into the water and waded over to hold it, a muscular, dense creature as heavy as a silver ingot, with blue iridescence flashing off its skin. I wanted to get a picture, shake Maitland's hand, and thank the Lord for this bonefish, which was one of the most beautiful creatures I'd ever seen. But first I thought I'd better get it back into the water.

Kneeling down in the tepid water, I moved the fish back and forth until its tail began to pump. As soon as it began to fight my grip, I let go. I felt a great surge of satisfaction as it flashed away.

"Thanks, Maitland," I said, shaking his hand.

He grinned, and gripped my hand. "Congratulations."

We climbed into the boat, and I slumped down into the seat, exhausted and relieved. Paul came wading through the shallows, smiling, holding up his camera to let me know he'd captured the scene. "Hop in there, captain," Maitland ordered him. "You're next."

||||||||||||||||||||||||||||||||||||||||||||||||||||||

The

WAITING GAME

◇◇◇◇◇

*N*ot long ago, my old friend Doug Allen was driving his water taxi down the river when a guy climbed over the railing on Winnipeg's Osborne Street Bridge and balanced there on the narrow ledge, getting ready to jump. He was a native guy, and as he gazed down at the muddy river, possibly mumbling a few last words to his Creator, traffic began to pile up and emergency sirens came whooping through the summer heat.

Doug flipped his boat in and out of gear, hanging in the current beneath the bridge, waiting to see if the man was actually going to do it. "The river is pretty shallow there," said Doug. "I think he would have lodged in the bottom like a lawn dart."

Doug watched cops and firefighters talk to the man, trying to persuade him to come back over the railing. "I was the only one with a boat," said Doug. "And the cops were giving me the thumbs up, like saying, stick around."

It was rush hour, and with one of Winnipeg's main bridges now shut down, horns blared everywhere and the whole central downtown was descending into gridlock. As a group of police officers kept the man distracted, Doug observed a lone firefighter creep toward the jumper, using the railing as cover. When the firefighter was close enough, he pounced, grabbing the guy around the neck and by the belt. A couple of cops leapt forward, seized the man, and flung him into the air, straight up over the railing and down onto the sidewalk.

"It was basically a World Wrestling Federation smackdown," Doug told me. "They face-planted this guy into the pavement, piled onto him, gave him the knee on the neck, the handcuffs, then fired him into the back seat of the squad car. It was pretty rough. If I was the jumper, I think I would have preferred taking my chances with the river."

He told me this a few days later, in the dining room of my house. It was a beautiful summer morning, and we were getting ready to go fishing. Rods and fishing tackle were spread out on the table, and I was making lunch, stuffing apples and sandwiches into the beat-up leather knapsack that I use for fishing trips.

We weren't going to some far-off wilderness destination. We were going fishing in the city. There are two big rivers, chock full of fish, running right through the middle of Winnipeg. They're also chock-full of flotsam, effluvium, discarded shopping carts, and an occasional dead body, but we didn't care. When guys get together, they like to do something active, something that requires tools or long sticks. Doug and I make a point of getting together once in a while, and today fishing was our excuse.

Outside, we climbed on our bikes, shouldered our backpacks, and glided down the street. The scent of lilacs was heavy in the air. Most of my tackle was at the lake, and we didn't even have bait. But it was one of those jade-green, dewy mornings when, with a good bike underfoot and your lunch on your back, you can't help but feel like Fortune's Favored Child. We had no precise idea where we were going, but there was no shortage of options. Winnipeg's two main rivers, the Assiniboine and the Red, are populated by about fifty species of fish, including silver bass, sauger, pike, sturgeon, and walleye. The most prized of the lot is the channel catfish, which grows to well over thirty pounds. We weren't fixated on catching a catfish that big. But tonight, when Doug and I concluded our safari with a cold beer, we hoped to be able to say that we'd at least caught a medium-sized one.

First order of the day was acquiring some bait. A lot of anglers think that you need something truly evil and smelly to attract a catfish. Down in the southern United States, where they used to think they had the best catfishing in the world, there's a long tradition of brewing up "stinkbaits" for cats. The idea is, you put chunks of liver or beef heart in glass bottles and place them out in the hot sun for a few weeks. The smell, when you open the lid, is allegedly sufficient to make a buzzard gag. But our northern, better-bred channel catfish seem to prefer fresh bait, like chunks of raw liver. Live frogs apparently work well, if you've got the heart to hook one. Hefty chunks of oily, fresh fish are even better. My acquaintance Stu McKay, who works as a professional guide on the Red River and who has probably caught more gigantic catfish than anyone in the province, likes using sections of Winnipeg goldeye, a delicate silvery species that looks like a small whitefish. Doug and I had none of the above, so we cycled over to Stephen & Andrew's gourmet food store to see if George had any tiger prawns on ice. When I told George that we were going to use them for bait, he was appalled. "You're going to waste these on a catfish?"

"If the catfish don't like them," said Doug, "we'll grill some for dinner."

Doug knows food, and he fancies himself a bit of a gourmand. His grandparents lived on a huge estate in Toronto, although in 1929 his family lost everything in the stock market crash. Doug's mother plucked the roses in the garden and put the petals in a Ming vase, a vase Doug still carries with him as he moves from one place to another. Doug's facility for a quip is legendary, and most people who know him think he would have made a top-notch courtroom lawyer. But with all that, he's fifty-six years old, drives a water taxi, and lives in a run-down triplex in a crime-ridden neighborhood. People sometimes ask me, with feigned concern, "What happened with Doug?" as if they detect an invisible cloud hovering over him. I tell them he's fine. What happened to Doug is life.

Stuffing the prawns into our backpacks, we mounted our bikes and carried on. The streets of Winnipeg are confusing to visitors. They wind and bend, constantly changing their names, making dogleg turns for no apparent reason and meeting at thronging, sign-plastered, five-way intersections that are bewildering to wend your way through if you don't know the moves. The streets wind and bend because of the city's rivers. Water flows through the city's history, and the root of its name, winnipi, is a Cree word meaning "muddy water." When Metis buffalo hunters settled here in the early 1800s, property lines and trails were laid out to conform to the paths of the Red and the Assiniboine. As Doug and I cycled west along the verdant avenue known as Wellington Crescent, the road followed the sinuous curves of the river. Every so often, we caught glimpses of water through the trees. Our idea was to go as far as we could reasonably go in the suburbs, then work our way back into the heart of the city, checking out likely spots along the way. It would be drive-by fishing.

Our first stop was a grassy meadow next to a footbridge crossing the river. I tied on a swivel, a leader, and a two-ounce slip sinker, then impaled a fat prawn on the needle-sharp Gamakatsu hook. With my first cast, I managed to hit an overhanging tree limb. My rig spun like a bola, wrapping itself around the branch so tightly that for years hence I'm sure it will dangle there, serving as yet another reminder of why people shouldn't litter. The naked branch was high above the river, so there wasn't much point in trying to persuade Doug to scale the tree and retrieve my precious twenty-five-cent sinker. He was busy anyway, walking up and down the riverbank, swearing to himself as he wrestled with his first snag.

I knelt on the grass and tied up another swivel, sinker, leader, hook, and bait, regretting that I hadn't brought a hat. Even though it was only mid-morning, the sun was working on my bald spot like a heat gun. Tying a red bandanna over my head, I walked along the riverbank with my new rig, took a cast, and immediately got snagged. When in the comfort of our homes we plan these jaunts, we tend to forget that fishing is one of the most annoying things you can do with your spare time.

After losing a couple of rigs each, Doug and I managed to get some baits deployed. We sat down on the grass with our rods, taking care not to disturb our accursed baits. Now we would wait. Fishing involves a lot of waiting. Ostensibly, you're waiting for a bite, but bites come so infrequently that you'd get bored very quickly if that was all you were waiting for. You're really just waiting in a general sense. You're sitting on the grass, watching an ant crawl along a stick, watching the brown river slide past. In nature, there's a general sense of portent. It's not likely that the river will reveal something. But if it happens, you'll be there.

Doug screwed the cap off his thermos and poured us each a cup of coffee. When he was a young guy, Doug bore a striking resemblance to the moppy-haired rock singer John Cougar Mellencamp. He drove a Triumph Bonneville, which is about the classiest motorcycle ever built, and certain kinds of young women almost squirmed when he sat down at the next table. I drove a wimpy little Honda trail bike and found girls hard to come by, so I observed these brazen females with disapproval.

Sometimes I would phone Doug late at night and he'd put me off, saying, "Can I call you tomorrow? I'm working on a hat trick." (A "hat trick" entails sleeping with three women in one day.) Even when he was middle-aged, women would sometimes walk up to him and ask him if there was someplace they could go. Now that he's in his late fifties, I don't think it's happened for a while. His hair is gray. His face is the face of an old sea dog, furrowed and weather-beaten from spending a lifetime by the water. There's usually a Player's plain drooping from the corner of his mouth, and his right eye is in a permanent squint from the smoke.

As we reclined in the sun, we noticed that, on the far side of the river, an animal was thrashing in the water. There's a lot of wildlife along the riverbank, and we wondered what kind of animal it was. Foxes, raccoons, and even lynx are frequently sighted, but this one looked like an aquatic mammal of some kind, maybe a beaver. As Doug and I watched, the beaver slowly turned into a man's head. His upper body emerged from the water, and he staggered a bit in the chest-deep river. "What in God's name is that guy doing?" Doug said.

I had no idea.

That Doug would witness two suicide attempts in less than a week seemed statistically unlikely. Given that the distant man seemed to be wearing one of those canary-yellow Tour de France cycling outfits, it seemed even less likely that he'd been drinking heavily. The reason for his struggles became apparent as he lifted a bicycle from the river and hefted it onto his shoulder. Struggling heroically, he climbed up through the willows and began ascending the steep cutbank. I noted the bicycle trails running along the top of the bank. "Maybe he was going too fast along the trail and didn't make the corner."

"That would have been quite a sight," Doug said. "Too bad we missed it."

The cyclist made it halfway up the cutbank, then lost his grip. The bicycle tumbled back into the river. He climbed down, entered the water, and retrieved the bike. For a good while we watched him repeat the process, climbing halfway up the bank, then fumbling the bike and dropping it into the river. We should have helped but couldn't. It was like watching a beetle trying to scale the inside of a bottle. No matter when you go fishing in the city, there's always some good sociology afoot. A few years ago, I was fishing not far from here when a passing canoeist overturned, then attempted to save his ratty little dog instead of his screaming girlfriend—no doubt what therapists would call "a defining moment in the relationship." After the cyclist had tackled his fourth or fifth Sisyphean climb, Doug reeled in a bit of line and discovered he was snagged again. "What the . . ."

"This place is bad luck," I said. "Let's roll."

Soon we were whirring, gliding, and tick-tick-ticking on our bikes through the forest. The bike trail scribed through the woods, swooping and curving as it followed the river. Beneath my front tire the packed mud was smooth, flanked by raised edges that resembled miniature grassy riverbanks. They've been here forever, these trails. Even when I was a kid they were part of the wooded landscape. Doug wouldn't have seen them because he grew up in Colombia, where his dad worked in an Imperial Oil drilling camp. Then Doug lived in Toronto, where a number of streets and parks are named after his ancestors. Eventually he moved to Winnipeg, where I met him in high school. I didn't really associate with him because he ran with a fast crowd. But later, when we both got married, we lived on the same street. Doug had settled down, and I'd wave to him in the morning as he went off in his suit and tie, the former bad dog now a bank manager.

He wasn't a fisherman in those days, but I introduced him to it. The first time he caught a bass, he got so excited that he swamped my canoe and we both nearly drowned. Later that day, canoeing back to our campsite, we were almost run over by a speedboat. That evening Doug blew up the Coleman stove and almost burned down our campsite. It was a memorable weekend, and we resolved to get out fishing more often. Twenty-five years have passed, and we're still doing it.

When you're hunting for channel catfish you watch the surface of the river, looking for ripples or whorls that suggest an irregularity in the river bottom. Catfish like to conserve energy by lying behind an obstruction in the current. They use their whiskers to sniff the passing water. If they catch a whiff of something edible, they'll move out and grab it. They monitor a fairly narrow zone, so it's a good idea to cast your bait toward a likely spot every ten minutes or so. Maybe a catfish will smell your bait, and maybe not. While you're waiting, you sit on the grass and watch the river.

Near the foot of Academy Road, I spotted a "seam" in the current, a place where the river bends and the water spins around into a back eddy. Fish of all kinds like seams. They'll line up where the two currents slide against each other and wait for the river to deliver something. Doug and I threw our baits into the seam and sat down, but we had no sooner gotten settled than some police scuba divers came working their way down the riverbank, groping in the muddy shallows. Doug knows all the local river gossip. He told me that the cops had found a severed arm a few days earlier and were probably looking for the rest of the body.

We watched them for a while, hoping they'd come up with the carcass, but they were combing the shallows with the dutiful motions of people who don't really expect to find anything. I told Doug about a police diver I used to know. Apparently you can't see anything down there. The cop told me that in the winter the divers sometimes get wedged between the ice and the river bottom. The ice presses down on your back and the mud bottom presses against your chest, and the current holds you in the narrowing. The cop told me one time he located a body under the ice and was towing it by the leg back to the hole they'd cut in the ice when the corpse came to life and grabbed him by the neck. It was his partner, playing a joke. "Good thing he didn't flip out and drown," Doug said. "That would have ruined the joke."

As the frogmen worked their way closer to our fishing spot, Doug and I realized they would scare off any catfish in the area. We reeled in and carried on.

A mile farther down the river, among the shady elms behind the Shaarey Zedek synagogue, we tossed out our baits again. Almost immediately, Doug had a bite. His rod tip gave a pronounced twitch, once, twice; then the catfish took off.

Doug opened the bail and let the fish run with the bait. This is the exciting part, watching the line peel off. Catfish live in lazy, slow-moving rivers, and anglers who are unfamiliar with them think they're lazy, slow-moving fish. This is incorrect. With their long, muscular bodies and dramatically forked tails, channel catfish are built for struggling against the never-ending force of the water. Unlike some species, they don't become oxygen deficient after a four-minute tussle. Endurance is their game, and after a fifteen-minute fight a catfish is fighting almost as hard as when it first hit the bait. Doug was well equipped, using a big surf-casting reel loaded with two hundred yards of twenty-five-pound line. As the line poured off the reel, he stood up and dug his feet in, getting ready for the mayhem that would erupt when he set the hook.

After counting to ten, he closed the bail, reared back and pulled the bait right out of the fish's mouth. He barked a profanity. I enthusiastically concurred.

This happens a lot with catfish. A few minutes later, I saw my own rod tip bobbing. It could have been the current, so I watched closely before I touched the rod. A river usually appears to be moving at a lazy pace. But it actually moves with a subtle pumping motion. In the springtime, I've seen the same phenomenon with sheets of meltwater flowing down an alleyway. You get these waves, tiny tsunamis that roll forward in rhythmic patterns. The centrifuge of the earth's gravity, the pulsing of sunlight, or maybe just the cohesiveness of flowing molecules makes water reluctant to move. When it does, it pushes forward with an arterial pulsing. When you're fishing in a river, your rod tip is always nodding up and down with the irregular beat. A particularly strong throb of current can look like a catfish bite.

After a couple of pronounced nods, my rod settled down.

But then it gave a sharp rap and the line started spooling off. "Catfish!" I exclaimed, standing up.

It's always tricky, knowing when to stop the fish's run and set the hook. I tend to be a little impatient, so I counted to fifteen. It was exciting to watch the line looping off my big spinning reel, accelerating as the beast headed downstream, but when I closed the bail and reared back I likewise pulled the hook from the fish's mouth.

"What is this?" Doug said. "Abbott and Costello?"

We continued downstream, whickering along the mud-packed bike path, gliding through pools of shade and lilac perfume. Lots of people were out strolling. The river was once regarded as a natural sewer. Houses turned their backs to the water, and a screen of foliage separated restaurants and public parks from the riverbank. Now the river is being reclaimed by the citizenry, many of whom use fishing rods as an excuse to sit by the water.

Most inner-city fishermen are low-income folks who can't afford a boat or a cottage. You don't need money or even a tackle box to enjoy the river on a sunny day. A strong rod and some improvised bait are enough to put you in business. At the Legislative Buildings, Doug and I fished for a while with a road laborer named Adam, who was stretched out like a big cat on a concrete pier. Adam's method was to hook an earthworm to catch a little bullhead, which he then cut up and used for bait. "I fish here every day," he said. "Sometimes until three in the morning. Mosquitoes don't bother me; they never have. Last night I caught a thirty-nine-inch catfish. I don't know how much it weighed, because I don't weigh them. I figure a thirty-pound catfish would be what, about six feet long?"

Fishing was slow today. We sat on the concrete abutment trading stories. A police patrol boat sped past, throwing a big wake, and Adam gave them the finger. "They always drive like that," he said.

After a while we were joined by Bill, a shops teacher carrying a cooler, a radio, and a folding chair. Bill told us he often got up at four in the morning, bought a cappuccino and a bagel, and fished until it was time to go to school. "It's so peaceful down here in the early morning. You can arrive in the cool of the nighttime and watch it slowly get light." A few mornings earlier, he'd caught a twenty-eight-pound and a thirty-pound catfish before sunrise. "Until I weighed the second one, I thought it was the same fish." He said he'd seen a few vagrants and winos, but no one ever gave him a hard time. "It's like a shared space down here. Everybody goes by the rule of live and let live."

After fishing for an hour or two without getting a catfish, or any other fish for that matter, Doug and I cycled a few more miles down the river to the Forks. The Forks is at the junction of the Red and the Assiniboine, but it's more than just the meeting place of two historic waterways. The Forks is a thronging public space. Here, on almost any summer afternoon, thousands of people wander: listening to live music, shopping for fresh produce, or sitting in the sun and watching the river slide by. Some, like Doug and I, carry fishing rods.

We crossed the old railway bridge that spans the Assiniboine, chained our bikes to a tree, climbed down a steep cutbank, and rigged up our rods. Here, on a mud spit, the currents of both rivers merge. Discarded wine bottles and tin cans protruded from the compressed strata of the riverbank like fossils, and a dead tree as gnarled and white as the thigh bone of a dinosaur made a bench from which we could watch our lines. A red-headed guy and his son were already working the spot. As anglers do, we introduced ourselves.

Doug passed the time by joking with Drew, who proudly informed us that he was seven years old. Doug likes kids. He's surprisingly knowledgeable about childhood medical issues, and when his ex-wife Nancy was pregnant, years ago, he used to sit with me during lunch and talk about muconium membranes and Braxton Hicks contractions and so forth, to the point where I began to lose my appetite. His son Marc was born at almost the same time as my daughter Caitlin, and Doug became the stereotype of the doting father, reading books on child rearing and wheeling his shopping cart, loaded to the hilt with disposable diapers, up and down the aisle. Nancy was a flight attendant, so Doug became a part-time househusband, a role that seemed to bring some satisfying focus to his life.

When our marriages simultaneously fell apart, we'd sometimes go to Minaki for the weekend and stay on my houseboat, Doug and I and Caitlin and Marc. If I wanted to slip out to a party on a Saturday night, Doug was always happy to stay home with the kids, watch the moon come up, and tell them stories. I never worried about my daughter's safety when she was in Doug's charge. Seeing him with the kids was like watching a British bulldog guarding a pair of baby ducks.

Then Nancy decided she wanted to start afresh, and that was that. Doug fought to maintain contact with Marc, but the courts ruled against him. He told me that anyone who thinks fathers and mothers have equal status as parents has never spent much time in the court system. Nancy took Marc, moved out west, and washed Doug out of her hair. He sent cards, letters, and Christmas presents to Marc through her lawyer, but received no notes in return. He believes that Marc's mother threw the presents in the garbage. Now twelve years have gone by, and he doesn't know where Marc is.

Many single mothers do a fabulous job raising their boys, but there's no substitute for having a father in your life. How many mothers, for example, would come down to this river-bank and waste an afternoon with their son catching catfish and throwing mudballs in the water? In compensation for his loss, Doug gets some satisfaction from playing with other people's kids, and he gave our new young fishing partner a few tips about side-arm throwing. Drew's father, Daryn, was a fit-looking guy about thirty-five years old. He said he was a sol-dier, a Princess Patricia's Canadian Light Infantryman with seventeen years of service in war zones like Iran, Iraq, and the Balkans. "There's some good fishing in Bosnia," he said. "We caught some nice rainbows on the fly, and I got spooled by a real big one. But it's such a dangerous place. One time the locals started yelling at me and waving their arms. Then I realized I was right in the middle of a minefield. I had to back out, carefully. It was terrifying. One false move and I could have been blown to pieces."

Daryn and Drew used to drive for hours to go fishing, but they don't bother anymore, because there is such excellent fishing right in the middle of the city. He said, "Last week we caught lots of catfish right at this spot," said Daryn. "We had lots of double-headers. When you get home from overseas, it really makes you feel lucky to be a Canadian. Everyone you meet on the river is friendly, and it's such a treat to be out-doors on a day like this."

While we talked, Drew clambered around the riverbank, throwing whatever he could lift into the water. His bom-bardment seemed to stir up some action, because a fish sud-denly struck my bait, and I reeled in a six-pound silver bass. A moment later Daryn caught one too, larger than mine. After admiring our catches, we released them. Minutes later, Drew caught a fish. He screamed and grunted while he battled it. Silver bass are a hard-fighting fish, and their readiness to bite makes them popular with kids.

The four of us stayed on that spot for a couple of hours, catching silver bass and swapping stories. Doug told us about the time he took the Queen and her retinue of footmen and Scotland Yard bodyguards on a late autumn tour of the river. The boat stalled during the trip, and they floated for quite a while on the frigid river. "That engine had worked fine all summer," Doug said. "But before the Queen arrived, the Yardies tore the boat apart, looking for bombs. I'm sure they screwed up the motor."

The next day the British newspapers made a great fuss over Doug's peccadillo. ("Queen Adrift on Frozen Canadian River!") Doug could be seen, looking chagrined, on the front page of various British tabloids, getting a distinctly non-amused look from Her Majesty as she climbed off his boat. My sister Mary Kate phoned me from Rome, saying that she'd seen the British papers and wanted to pass on a message: "Way to go, Doug. You ruined the Queen's visit to Canada."

By early evening, we'd caught about a dozen fish. But none had whiskers.

Going home without catfish slime on our hands seemed a bit disgraceful, so Doug and I carried on. Midnight found us many miles downstream, at the place where the Red River thunders through the control gates of the Lockport dam. Anglers are often lined up along the catwalk beneath the dam, so even at this hour we weren't surprised to see a couple of fishermen working the night shift, sitting in folding chairs with their feet up on the rail. We joined them, introduced ourselves, and found out that their campaign to catch a bruiser of a channel catfish wasn't going any better than ours.

"I think they've been gorging on mayflies," said a guy named Nathan, gesturing up at the millions of bugs swirling around the mercury vapor lights above the dam. "The last couple of days have been real slow."

Doug and I tossed our baits into the river and started up with the usual Q & A. Anglers belong to a roughly knit family. It took Nathan and me only a few minutes to determine that we'd both guided for the same arctic fishing lodge and slept in the same bunkhouse, albeit twenty years apart. As we talked, the river pounded through slats in the dam and swirled beneath us, covered with a latte-brown froth. We leaned against the railing, swapping fish stories. After a few minutes, a fish hit my bait, hard, and stormed off downstream. I followed it, walking along the concrete manway, and soon landed a handsome, fork-tailed channel catfish.

At seven or eight pounds, it definitely wasn't a Master Angler trophy. But it was an indicator that the fishing might improve over the next few hours. In the heat of summer, channel catfish bite best at night. Some catfish anglers don't even bother fishing in the daytime.

After releasing the fish, I put on a fresh shrimp and tossed it to where an eddy formed a seam in the current. Leaning against the railing, I listened to Doug as he gave me the update on Marc. Recently, Marc had turned eighteen, the legal age at which he can make up his own mind about things, and Doug was hoping that one of these days the phone would ring. "I hope he understands that I've been waiting for years to talk to him. I don't even know what he looks like."

I remembered the six-year-old boy who used to sit beside Doug in the boat, grinning as if he'd won the jackpot when he reeled in a fish. I couldn't imagine what Marc looked like nowadays either—perhaps six feet tall, with a mop of hair like his old man.

Doug poured a couple of coffees and handed me one. In the gleam of the dam lights, the brown current churned and swirled, hiding its mysteries. It was late. But we stuck it out, leaning against the rail. We knew there was no point in getting impatient with the river.

Muskies

AND LIES

◇◇◇◇◇

*I*n fishing, as in life, certain rituals gather weight just because you do them every year. For twenty-six years, my fishing partner Dave Schneider and I have been getting together with a group of old friends and participating in a two-week-long fishing contest called the Bryant Cup Muskie Hunt.

When I was a young man, I worked as a fishing guide at a wilderness resort in Minaki. Most of my guests were American walleye fishermen. The average walleye is about the size of a tennis shoe. Walleyes are good to eat, but they are sulky, sluggish critters, and fishing for walleye is sometimes as exciting as spending eight hours straight playing "Button, button, who's got the button?" At the end of a long day on the water I'd clean my catch and then retire to the bar, where the conversation often turned to more exciting prey, like Esox masquinongy, the mythical muskellunge.

Muskies were supposedly abundant in my local waterway, the Winnipeg River. But other than the truly monstrous specimen mounted above the fireplace in the resort bar, I'd never seen one. Muskellunge are one of the largest predatory fish in fresh water. They grow to be well over four feet long, and over drinks the old guides told us stories of monster muskies that ate muskrats, loons, even small dogs. I often tried persuading my guests to lay off the walleyes and spend a day trying to catch a muskie. But the so-called "fish of ten thousand casts" is an elusive beast, and most tourists have no stomach for casting heavy lures for eight hours straight with nothing to show for it but a sore arm. Occasionally, some steely-eyed muskie hunter would show up in Minaki, carrying a rod as thick as a pool cue and a suitcase-sized tackle box full of lures. But serious muskie fishermen didn't tend to go out with punks like me.

Anybody who was serious about getting qualified as a muskie guide had to learn on his own time. In the evenings, I sometimes went looking for muskies with a fellow guide named Frank. Frank was a beefy, poker-faced guy with a Fu Manchu mustache. He liked painting and he loved fishing. We'd take my freighter canoe and go casting for muskies around the sunken docks, weedbeds, and rocky shoals where they were reputed to live. While we fished, Frank provided narration. As his lure came spluttering back through the lilypads, he'd intone, "The little duckling was a stranger to the savage ways of the weedbed." Then his voice would drop to an ominous baritone. "Suddenly the water erupted in a geyser of fury!"

At least once during the evening he'd shoot a finger at the water and gasp, "Look!!!" It was a joke that never failed to make my heart skip a beat. One night when he pulled the trick I refused to bite. An instant later, an enormous swirl appeared on the water. For days afterward, Frank talked about the huge muskellunge that had snapped at his lure and just missed. I would have seen it too, right there beside the boat, if only I'd looked.

The other guides were also chasing muskies in their spare time, but they weren't having any better luck. In the tradition of Sherlock Holmes, we were all proceeding deductively, figuring out what worked by eliminating what didn't. By the end of that first summer I still hadn't seen a muskellunge. But Frank had caught a thirty-pounder, which made me jealous enough to spend the winter daydreaming about muskies and reading whatever literature I could find. I learned that the muskellunge goes by many aliases—great blue pike, piconeau, silver tiger, and dozens more. Even the name "muskellunge" can undergo various phonetic spellings in the same textbook. Scientists suspect that the fish originated in Eurasia eons ago, crossing the sea by swimming through the layer of fresh water that covered the surface of the ocean during the melting of the glaciers. Once in North America, muskies migrated up the Mississippi and into the now long-gone Lake Agassiz. When the glacial meltwater receded, the fish became landlocked in a few lakes and rivers of the Great Lakes region, and there they remain today.

In Canadian history, the first mention of the species occurs in the Jesuit Relations, which refer to a great fish called the maskinonge, an Ojibwa name based on the words "mas" for ugly and "kinonge" for fish. During the 1890s, sporting journals like the *American Angler* began featuring stories about the huge and fearsome "muscalinga fish." One frustrated journalist of that Victorian era described the muskellunge as "a cross between a slinky alligator and a cunning woman." Another described the muskie as a sort of underwater Bolshevik that needed to be hunted down and terminated without mercy. "The muskie kills and maims ruthlessly. I have always believed that a bounty should be paid for big muskies. Their appetites are voracious. Often they kill for the sheer fun of it. And the destruction they can do in an hour is appalling."

Rookie anglers swallowed these stories, approaching muskie fishing as warfare. A gaff, a sawed-off pool cue, and a hip-mounted .22 pistol were basic equipment, and the most satisfying part of any fishing expedition involved stringing up the slain muskie for a photo opportunity. Numerous small towns laid claim to being the "muskie capital of the world," and giant muskies were a macabre tourist attraction. Tavern owners in Wisconsin and along the St. Lawrence River adorned the walls of their barrooms with big muskellunge, and millions of tourist dollars ebbed and flowed with the latest reported capture of a world-record fish. In Wisconsin, an innkeeper named Louis Spray resolved to make his own tavern more profitable by catching a giant muskie for the wall. He told his friends he firmly believed that if he fished every day of the season for five years, he could catch a new world-record.

On an October night in 1949, Spray delivered on his promise. He hooked a huge muskie in the Chippewa Flowage, near Hayward, Wisconsin, and subdued it after a forty-five-minute struggle. In a memoir he later penned about the adventure, Spray recalled: "We stopped at Charlie Pastika's bait shop but he had no scales. We stopped at Stroner's store, but his grocery scales would not weigh it either, so we went down to Karl Kahmann's. He showed me where the road became plugged with cars the last time the word got out that he had a big fish. They tore up his lawn, backed over his shrubbery, and did untold damage to his grounds. Karl said, 'Get that goddamn thing out of here and don't come back.'"

Spray and his cronies hauled the dead beast over to the local post office, where a postmaster finally agreed to weigh it on his government scale. The postmaster certified the muskellunge at sixty-nine pounds, eleven ounces. Given that the fish undoubtedly had lost weight as it dried out, it must have weighed well over seventy pounds alive. Gossip and exaggeration are so normal to muskie fishing that even with the physical evidence on hand, in the form of a great big slack-jawed dead fish, everyone still believed that Spray was lying. Tony Burmek, a local guide, told a reporter that he'd been fishing the reef where Spray allegedly caught the muskie and hadn't seen any other boats there.

Still, Spray must have caught the fish somewhere, so his rivals theorized that he'd taken it by foul play. The fish had been shot twice in the head, common practice while landing a muskie in those days. But rumor suggested that Spray had shot it when it swam past in shallow water. He and his friends countered with sworn affidavits that backed up his original story. Other guides came forward to testify that Tony Burmek was the damn liar, not Louis Spray, because they'd seen Burmek fishing four miles away from the spot where he claimed he was. Burmek proposed that everybody take a lie detector test to settle the matter once and for all, but Spray never showed up for the test. The balance of evidence was in Spray's favor, however, and the fish was recognized as a new world record. Fishing historians have never settled the matter. Spray might indeed have been lying in order to protect his secret spot. But since everybody would have expected him to lie, he might also have been telling the truth in an attempt to throw them off.

Anyone who reads the literature of muskie fishing soon learns that mendacity is woven into the very fabric of the sport. The postwar muskie fishing era was dominated by two

married couples. Between them, the Hartmans and the Law-
tons racked up twenty-five muskies weighing between fifty
and sixty pounds. Dozens of magazine articles celebrated
their angling prowess. In 1991, fishing experts began to suspect that the weight of the Hartmans' fish had been faked.
They confronted Len Hartman, who admitted in a videotaped
confession that he often filled the stomachs of his muskies
with wet sand and water, thereby adding as much as twenty
pounds to their weight.

Once the Hartman fish were disqualified, Art Lawton
became the champion of the world. His sixty-nine-pound,
fifteen-ounce muskie supposedly had been caught in the St.
Lawrence River in 1957. But a fishing historian with friends
in the right places subjected photographs of Lawton's record-
breaking muskie to forensic analysis in an FBI photo lab, and
he determined that the fish was much smaller than Lawton
had claimed—probably about forty-nine pounds. A photograph of another big fish suggested that Lawton had stuffed
something in its stomach, possibly a lead window weight.
The Freshwater Fishing Hall of Fame in Wisconsin—which
features an enormous statue of a muskellunge on its front
lawn—struck down Lawton's record and reinstated the fish
that Louis Spray had caught back in 1949. Today, Louis Spray
is considered the least outrageous of the various liars, and his
muskie is accepted as the official record.

As time went by, Frank and I and the other young guides
in Minaki learned that the best source of trusty information
was the local old-timers. The leading authority was an Ojibwa 129
fishing guide named George Kelly. In his prime, George was
so strong that he could carry two twenty-horse motors, one in
each hand, across a mile-long portage without once putting
them down. The American sportsmen who fished in Minaki

every summer so admired George that they'd invite him down to Chicago sports shows in the winter, where he'd entertain the crowds with his storytelling and his ability to carry enormous loads of flour. When I began fishing in Minaki, George was approaching the end of his guiding career. He was a living encyclopedia of the best techniques and places to fish for muskies. But George didn't go around dispensing grandfatherly advice. He was a sly man, and if you asked him a question about fishing he'd flash a wolfish grin and answer with a joke or a riddle.

George wasn't interested in giving away his muskie fishing secrets. But my friend and fellow guide Dave Schneider pestered George constantly, and George finally agreed to take us fishing in return for a case of beer. George used a lot of bizarre techniques, which were either brilliant or absurd. He would approach a fishing spot at high speed, circle around it repeatedly, gun the motor, and then stop the boat and slap the water with a paddle, over and over again, with such vigor that the sound echoed like gunshots off the nearby cliffs. Then Dave and I tossed lures while George drank beer and watched. We tried three spots, but no muskies appeared. At the last spot, George once again slapped the paddle on the water, then dropped the anchor overboard and bounced it on the bottom.

"Don't just sit there, get casting," he said with his trademark wink, a half-comic expression that always made you suspect a joke was going down at your expense. Dave cast his bucktail first, and the blade hadn't revolved more than two or three times when an enormous, tiger-striped muskie rose from the depths and smashed the lure so hard that it flew through the air. Dave retrieved the lure (with its bent treble hooks) and we both cast frantically for several minutes, hoping the muskie would return. But it was gone, and George was laughing. "I oughta hit you with the paddle," he said. "C'mon, reel in. We're going home."

The last time I saw George, he was limping along on a pair of crutches. He was wearing a pith helmet, pajamas, and a pair of plush bedroom shoes designed to resemble beer cans. He looked feeble, but he had a gleam in his eye that you could see from fifty feet away. He told me that he'd escaped from the local old folks' home and was looking for a place where he could meet a woman and get a drink. I talked to him for a few minutes and wished him luck. He walked a few steps and then stopped, shook an ominous finger in my direction. "Before I die," he said, "I want to take you and Dave out one more time and show you how to catch those muskies." I meant to take him up on it, but I wasn't quick enough. A short while later George died, taking all his secrets with him.

Another grizzled veteran was Doug Bryant. He was a big man with the thick arms and rounded shoulders of a grizzly, and every night, down at the filleting shack, he would entertain us with tales of the giant muskies he'd seen that day. With Doug's encouragement, I kept going after muskies, and one hot August night I finally caught one. At six pounds it wasn't a big fish, but it was a genuine muskellunge. And as I released the fish, I felt that I could finally call myself a muskie angler.

The following year, Doug drowned in a boating accident. Gary Lovett (better known as "Guide Brown," or simply "Browner") decided to launch an annual fishing derby in Doug's honor. Browner, a jaunty individual with a weathered baseball hat cocked atop his head, moved to appoint himself Dictator for Life, and seconded the motion to make it law. Although also a rookie guide, Browner was an accomplished angler who already had dozens of muskies under his belt. He knew Doug better than any of us did, and I assumed that Doug had taught him a lot of his tricks. Browner disabused me of that, however, explaining that Doug was a better story-teller than fisherman. "Doug couldn't catch a muskie to save his life," said Browner. "But he was a great guy. The derby is named after him because he was the first one to die."

The young guides are now much older and we have scat-tered to the four winds, but we return to compete in the Bry-ant Cup Muskie Hunt every August. No one wants to be the first to break the spell. Johnny Coke, the banking executive, bails out of a plane from Toronto. Doug Eastwood comes winging in from Edmonton. Rupe Ross slips off his Crown prosecutor's robe, slips on his red lumberjacket, and points his boat north toward the seagull-whitened reef that bears his name. Nine Fingers Phil, nowadays better known as Dr. Carter, appears on the crest of a hill, pensively twirling his mustache with what's left of his fingers.

Over time, the local muskies have become characters in their own right. Most big muskies are females, and Bernice is one of the biggest. She lives in the channel near Birch Island. Long and slender, Bernice weighed in at over thirty pounds when she was first caught five years ago. She has only been subdued once since then, as far as we know, but judging from her occasional appearances Bernice is alive and well and still growing. If we're casting near Birch Island and something as long and sinuous as an anaconda appears behind our lure, we know it's her.

132 Old Jingles is another famous local. She's an enormous beast, generally considered large enough to break the world record. Seen at various times by members of the Hunt, Old Jingles has achieved legendary status. One of the hunters was tussling with a ten-pound northern pike one evening when the

fish suddenly panicked and jumped into the boat. A muskie the size of an alligator abruptly rolled and turned away. Browner is one of the many who have seen Old Jingles up close. "I would swear, quite seriously, that she's eight feet long," he declares. "But I know that's impossible. So let me put it this way. I've seen lots of forty-pounders, and she's twice as big."

Even for those who haven't seen her, Old Jingles haunts the imagination. Huge as a railway tie, scarred, maned with moss and frayed fishing line, the big muskie supposedly has so many walleye spinners and tiny rusty bass lures hanging from her jaw that she jingles like a carriage horse when she crashes out of the water.

To win the Bryant Cup, a team usually has to chalk up six or seven good muskies. The Dictator often sets a good example by catching more than anyone. Most participants have work and family obligations, and they're quite happy to get out casting five or six evenings during the derby, maybe catching one fish a year, just so that they can show their faces at the wind-up dinner. On the evening of the last day, we gather for speeches, jokes, and the awarding of the Bryant Cup. Everyone stands on the lawn for a group photo. Earlier versions of that same photograph are posted on the wall of the clubhouse. It's like viewing an experiment in time lapse photography. Some of the participants have died or drifted away. But it's amusing to see how many of the faces reappear, their cowboy boots and long hair gradually transforming into sensible shoes and a bald spot.

After all these years of muskie fishing I still haven't caught a real monster, which is usually considered to be a fish of thirty pounds or more. But I still like to make sure I'm in Minaki during the Bryant Cup tournament so that I can sign up for the hunt and give it a shot.

133

At the worst, you get to see old friends and attend a great party, with thick barbecued T-bones and a lot of fifty-year-olds jiving to the Rolling Stones on the lawn. And who knows? I've had a lot of bad luck with muskies, but luck can always change. If you get out there, night after night, there's always a chance of catching Old Jingles.

Jacks or
BETTER TO OPEN

◇◇◇◇◇

*I*t was daybreak in the Bahamas, and the bustling crowds and echoing flight announcements inside Nassau International Airport would have seemed more festive if it hadn't been such a dark and rainy morning.

Steve Alsip and I had gotten soaked on the way to the airport. Now, while we stood around drinking bad coffee and trying to dry off, the airline clerk in the departure lounge kept giving us regretful looks, as if preparing to tell us our flight was canceled. We'd more or less resigned ourselves to getting rained out when our pilot—a wiry black man in an impeccably creased uniform—walked into the lounge. Looking us up and down, he gestured for me and Steve and the two other passengers to follow him outside. With a cloud ceiling of only a few hundred yards and rain billowing sideways down the tarmac, it was a bad day for flying. But we were itching to go, and this pilot was just the sort of lunatic we'd been hoping for.

Along with the other passengers—evangelical missionaries of the Lord, judging by their Bibles and clothing—Steve and I humped our gear out to the Navajo aircraft and climbed aboard. Minutes later, our pilot pressed the throttles to the firewall and we roared down the runway. As the plane shook itself free of the earth and climbed into the rain, Steve squinted at me, smiled, and gave me a thumbs-up. At last, we were on our way.

Our destination was a fishing lodge on the island of Andros, which lies about thirty miles west of Nassau. As we flew west, I gazed down at the dark, wind-wrinkled sea. This was a Visual Flight Rules (VFR) flight, so the pilot was staying beneath the clouds. If we ran into heavy rain, we'd be screwed. If we crashed into that water down there, they'd never find us, because this strait—the Tongue of the Ocean— is more than a mile deep.

The United States Navy operates an experimental under-sea weapons project in the Tongue. Apparently navy divers occasionally run into bizarre deepwater creatures like the oarfish, an almost transparent, hundred-foot-long fish that swims vertically, like a seahorse, and has the quilled mane and bulging eyes of a sea monster. When startled, the oarfish folds its fins and spirals down into the abyss, which is pretty much what we would do if this old plane smacked the water. In the black depths of the Tongue, our bodies would never decay. We'd sit buckled into our seats for eternity, staring out the window at the luminous creatures drifting by. On a morning like this, it didn't sound like such a bad fate for a couple of long-time fishermen.

As we drew closer to Andros, the pilot eased back on the throttles and we descended through murk, bouncing and slewing in the rough air. The missionaries behind us clutched their hands. "Lord save us!" quailed the man of the duo, who had lavishly oiled hair and the abbreviated mustache of a burlesque-house piano player. I gave up praying long ago, but I would gladly take it up again if there was any evidence that God, if there is one, saves or condemns us based on how avidly we cringe when we're about to get a licking.

Steve, who in middle age is still as fearless as a juvenile delinquent, was chewing gum and reading an instruction manual for apprentice fly fishermen. Steve and I have fished together all our lives. When we were young and poor, we used to go on camping trips and cast for pike from my beat-up old freighter canoe. When Steve became a successful lawyer, we would cast for channel catfish from the riverbank behind his plush home in Winnipeg. Now that I'd taken up fly-fishing, I was hoping to convert him. It's a part of my lifetime task to try and drag Steve up, morally, and it's his to drag me down. I think his job is the more entertaining.

"Look at this dork," he said, showing me the book. On the dust jacket was a photograph of the author, who was standing in a stream proudly displaying a miniature trout. The author was wearing a multipocketed vest and one of those snap-brimmed hats meant to suggest that the wearer is part Harvard MBA and part Australian outlaw. "Who'd take a picture of that fish?" Steve chuckled, stuffing the book in the seat pocket. He looked out the window. "Holy shit, look at those clouds."

As the plane took a particularly violent bounce, the missionaries yelped. We were supposed to be landing in a little settlement called Congo Town, but we could barely see the ground. The pilot kept swooping lower, and patches of wind-wracked jungle flashed beneath us. He circled the airport twice and then, with another squall closing in, evidently opted for the old bush pilot's dictum ("When in doubt,

137

chicken out") and hammered the engines. Ten minutes later, we approached the alternate airport of Mangrove Cay, where the storm slackened long enough to allow for a steep descent and a walloping landing. Steve and I hauled our fishing gear across the flooded tarmac. It felt good to walk on solid asphalt. At least for today, fishing wasn't going to be the death of us.

Loading our gear into a taxi, we headed off down a gravel road. Andros, 140 miles from top to bottom, is the largest island in the Bahamas. An immense coral reef surrounds the island and makes shipping traffic impossible, so the population has remained more or less static for centuries. There's only one rough road linking the island's widely spaced villages. As we bounced past little communities of cinderblock shacks and junked automobiles, we might as well have been cruising through some scruffy region of West Africa.

When we arrived at Moxey's Bonefishing Lodge, Steve and I were greeted by its owner, Joel Moxey, a well-dressed black man with the suave manner of a bank manager, which in fact he once was. Joel showed us our rooms and then introduced us to Ezra Gray, who was going to be our guide. We told Ezra we were keen to hit the water. Ezra, a tall goateed man who spoke with the gravity of an actor playing Othello, said it was probably a complete waste of time to try fly-fishing in this wind, but he agreed to take us out for a few hours. Steve and I changed into dry pants and carried our tackle down to the water.

The beach was an expanse of gray muck. The shoreline was littered with heaps of rotting conch shells and derelict fishing boats. On one of these overturned skiffs, three wild-eyed men were having an argument, talking in loud shouts and waving their arms with the theatricality of the seriously drunk. Once they spotted us, they gesticulated fran-

138

tically. Steve walked over. Just as some people shy away from trouble, Steve is drawn to it. "What's with all the noise?" he shouted at them.

Here we go, I thought. We've only arrived and already it's starting. I resisted the urge to nag Steve and instead waded out to Ezra's skiff, wincing as my bare feet sank into the malodorous mud and jagged shells.

"Give me your rod, sir," said Ezra.

I was standing beside the boat, knee deep in water. I carefully handed him my eight-hundred-dollar Orvis fly rod. Over the years I've broken at least half a dozen of them, and I hoped to make this one last. Ezra handled the rod as if it were a piece of stemware. He stowed it in the rod locker, then murmured, "What is your friend's name, sir?"

"Steve."

Back on the beach, Steve was encircled by the drunks. I gripped the gunwales and hefted myself, kicking my feet to sluice off the muck, then clambered into the boat. It was a clean skiff, and Ezra was putting everything in its proper place. He handed me a wet towel and I wiped the seat. Steve came slopping out to the boat. His pants were rolled up and he was grinning like a jack-o'-lantern. "What did you do, give them money?" I asked.

He nodded. "Twenty bucks. I made them promise to spend it on liquor."

When Steve was a lawyer, he was always befriending his criminal clients. His law office was in an old mansion in downtown Winnipeg. I seldom visited him during office hours, because like most lawyers he was too busy yelling into his speaker phone. But when I did drop over there to meet him for lunch or to get his opinion on some incomprehensible contract, his waiting room was full of men who looked as if they were impersonating the characters from *The Wind in the Willows*. Long-haired drug dealers, sneak thieves, bleary-eyed salesmen who'd flunked the breathalyzer: they were all waiting to see their pal Steve.

There was even a room next to the furnace that Steve sometimes "rented" to his more desperate clients. If they couldn't get Legal Aid to pay their bills they'd offer Steve barter. He usually couldn't accept it, because everything they owned was stolen. When one of Steve's clients, a prominent restaurateur and well-known cokehead, was arrested and sent to jail, the cops for some reason gave Steve a loot bag full of the man's personal weapons. Steve gave me one of the pistols. (Hey, thanks, Steve!) I had fun shooting tin cans and devising secret hiding places for it around the house until a precocious redheaded girl who lived next door to Steve broke into his house and made off with one of the larger guns, a hefty, nickel-plated .357 revolver, which she took into the back yard and tested on various trees, waking the neighborhood with the crash-bang of the reports.

The cops arrived at Steve's door—the same detectives who'd given him the guns in the first place—and threatened to charge him with possession of restricted weapons. He sat them down in his kitchen and pointed out that charging him might not be a smart career move. After all, what kind of police officers were they to give restricted guns to someone like him? He recommended they come up with a cover story. The police officers thought this over and saw his logic. But they insisted they wanted all the guns back. So I dropped my poor little Smith & Wesson into a brown paper bag and took it to the police station, where one of the detectives palmed it as calmly as if I were delivering a bagel.

Washing the muck off his feet, Steve climbed into the boat. He stowed his knapsack in the forward hatch, then lit a butt and sat down beside me. Ezra started the motor and cruised out of the harbor. Steve flicked his cigarette ash in the water and looked at me. "Are we fishing with normal rods or Martha Stewart rods?"

"Why don't you try the fly rod? See if you like it."

"Will I catch more fish with it?"

"Just give it a chance."

Ezra fed some gas to the big Yamaha and we sped up, bumping across the waves. The coastline fell off to our left. To the right was the choppy, charcoal-gray expanse of the Tongue of the Ocean. Steve looked around, taking it all in. When he's smiling, which is often, his face creases up like one of those Chinese temple dogs. His hair is multidirectional and disarrayed. On his right cheek is a blurry scar, a memento of the time his brother lit him on fire.

I've known Steve since we were teenagers, but I've had to rely on stories from his brothers and sisters and his mother, Squeezey Louise, for tales about his boyhood. One time, for example, Steve was hopping cars in the winter when a delivery truck drove right over him. He went home, urinating blood, and didn't tell anyone. Louise eventually found out when she noticed the snow-tire marks on his chest. Another time he climbed Queenston School on a twenty-five-cent dare. When he reached the roof, he slipped off and plummeted three stories to the pavement.

When my daughter Caitlin was young she always used to peer out the window when we drove past. "Is that the school that Steve fell off?" I can hardly drive past it myself without thinking, boy, that's high. It's a good forty-foot drop to the asphalt. On the way down Steve decided to land stiff-legged, which saved his skull at the expense of his legs. He shattered his feet and left what he described as "an incredible explosion of snot" on the asphalt.

Now he's fifty-four years old, lives in Nassau and sells sex products through the mail. When I pry into his business affairs, asking him how much money he makes, he can barely keep a straight face. "I can't tell you."

"Stamp your right hoof if it's more than four hundred K."

"Get fucked. Do you think I'd leave my law practice and come down here for that kind of chump change?"

"Well, that's nice, but I hope you're putting some of it into a retirement plan."

"Not a cent."

"One day you're going to wake up and you'll be out of money."

He laughs heartily. "Not much chance of that."

I used to see Steve all the time when he lived in Winnipeg. But five years have gone past since he left, and this fishing trip is a trumped-up excuse to get together.

After Ezra had driven several miles up the coast, he slowed the boat and we pulled into a wide bay. It was still raining and our clothes were soaked. "Good bonefish spot," Ezra said. "This is your first time with the fly rod, sir?"

"I'm afraid so," Steve answered. "And call me Steve."

"Yes, sir."

Guides in the Bahamas like to maintain a certain formality with their guests. I've tried getting friendly with them, but they prefer to call you "sir." You have to accept that you're not their friend. You might be from the mainland; you might be a member of the Caucasian ruling class and have more money than they do. But out here on the water, you can't tie knots, you can't spot fish, and you can't cast. Insisting that your Bahamian guide address you by your first name is equivalent to suggesting that you're equals, and you're not.

Ezra opened the rod locker and delicately removed a fly rod for Steve. "Let's have a look at your flies."

· "I don't have any."

"He'll use mine," I said, giving Ezra my tackle box. Ezra picked through the box and selected a fly. Then he showed Steve how to tie a nail knot. Ezra did this deftly and quickly, although most people find the nail knot maddeningly difficult to execute even when comfortably seated at a dining room table. Testing the nail knot with a tug of his muscular arms, Ezra next showed Steve how to join the three sections of tippet (using the even more maddening blood knot) and how to tie a fly onto the tippet using the double clinch knot. ("Wrapped only five times, sir, not six. Each extra wrap makes the knot a little bit weaker.") Then Ezra stepped up onto the platform, tore eighty feet of line off the reel, and unfurled several long graceful casts. "Like that, sir," he murmured. "You don't have to throw it hard. It's in the timing."

He handed the rod to Steve. "You try it, sir."

Steve took the rod and whipped it back and forth, looking as if he was trying to kill a swarm of gnats. Ezra stepped in, took the rod, and once again demonstrated the right technique. Ezra was clearly one of those natural athletes who can shoot the line as straight as an arrow but can't explain how he does it. Steve is one of those guys who makes an attempt at listening to directions but secretly thinks that if something is worth knowing he would already know it. If a female anthropologist had been with us, carrying a clipboard and wearing a white lab coat, she no doubt would have been scribbling observations of this tense and classic "guy" moment—Ezra mumbling vague instructions, Steve pretending to listen, and me, afraid to say anything lest I be told to shut the fuck up, crouching on the floor of the boat as hooks whistled past my head.

After a few hours of fruitless casting, we headed back to the lodge, skunked and soaked. At the beach, the bums were waiting patiently for Steve. After an obligatory round of handshakes and boozy affirmations of everyone's integrity, we walked up to the lodge, eager to get out of our wet clothes and hit the shower.

At Moxey's Lodge, dinner is served in a little room next to the kitchen. Moxey's is not a fishing resort, it's a fishing lodge. At a fishing resort, you sit in a tastefully appointed dining room, sipping merlot and listening to mellow jazz while the fireplace crackles. At a fishing lodge, you sit at a plywood table off the kitchen and wolf down whatever the women in the kitchen throw on your plate. Your dinner companions might be millionaires or truck drivers, but you don't know the difference because everyone has the same bad hair and windburned face. Nobody cares what anyone else does for a living, anyway. They just want to know what you caught that day, which in our case was nothing.

After dinner Steve and I walked down the mosquito-infested road, past the junked cars and heaps of rotting conch shells, to call our sweethearts from the village's only functioning telephone. A pair of starving dogs circled me, growling, while Steve used the phone. Another benefit of staying at a fishing lodge, as opposed to a resort, is that you can stand there and wave off the mosquitoes and say, "Honey, you wouldn't like it here," and actually be telling the truth.

Returning to the lodge, Steve and I had drinks with the other guests. They came from three or four different countries. The world is small, for anglers, and it turned out that we'd fished in many of the same rivers and lakes. One of them, a Brit named Martin James, worked for the BBC and had even fished the Red River in Winnipeg, where he claimed to have caught bigger catfish than either Steve or I had. Steve and I didn't believe him, but sadly, Martin had the pictures.

The walls of the bar were covered with fading black-and-white photographs. As he pointed out the various characters in the photographs, Joel Moxey told us that his family got started in the fishing business about fifty years ago, when the wealthy Mellon family came to Andros and employed Joel's dad and his uncle as their guides. Over the years, legendary anglers like Lefty Kreh, Curt Gowdy, and Chico Fernandez discovered the Moxey family and helped turn them into notables in their own right.

One of the pictures showed Joel's Uncle James, who is still a respected bonefish guide although he is stone deaf and eighty-eight years old. Another showed a gnarled old guide named John Wayne Moxey, standing waist-deep in water, holding up a barracuda almost six feet long. Slack-jawed and jaggedly toothed, the barracuda looked like a hound from hell. Large barracuda are considered inedible because they often cause ciguatera poisoning. Or at least that's what I've heard. For that reason, many anglers decline to eat them, although Ansil Saunders, the famous Bimini guide, once told me that he still enjoys a pan-fried barracuda steak now and then, even though his dad got ciguatera and had to be tied to the bed because he wanted to tear his own eyes out. Fly anglers like barracudas, despite their shortcomings as table fare, because they readily take a fly and go completely ballistic when hooked. As Joel pointed out, "They can sprint up to forty-five miles per hour, which makes them one of the fastest fish in the world."

Moxey's Lodge has no temptations to keep a man up past bedtime, so we retired at a good hour. Lying in our bunks, Steve and I talked like boys in the dark. Steve wanted to know how things were going with "the blonde," as he describes Ann, my girlfriend. Ann is an uptown girl, an executive editor at a big-city magazine, and in many ways there couldn't be two people more incompatible than her and Steve. When I first introduced them, at a lawn party, I feared there would be some kind of caustic explosion. But she told me afterward that although she despised the cruel way Steve talked about animals and women, he was the only one of my friends that she could imagine running away with.

I told Steve that Ann was fine and asked him how things were going with his twenty-eight-year-old black girlfriend, Dominique, whom he calls the Dominator.

He said he'd settled down a lot, and life was quiet. In the morning he and Dominique usually played some nude Scrabble before breakfast; then they played golf or drank cocktails. There is lots of money in Nassau. Peter Nygaard has the world's biggest private residence on a nearby point of land, and Sean Connery lives just down the road. Steve's friends include people like Jim Frew, a snowy-haired retired USAF general who has written several successful adventure novels. ("They're not really novels," he told me. "They're just stories I make up in my head.") I also met the Pro, Steve's best friend, a bar owner who used to be the Dirty Harry of the Royal Bahamas Police Force. The Pro, according to Steve, "shot plenty of guys" when he was on the job. The drug dealers would come out of the airplane with their hands up, and the Pro would let them have it with the Kalashnikov. In person, the Pro isn't intimidating. He's an average-sized black guy with a straight handshake and a polite manner. But if you mention his name in any bar in Nassau you get a wary chuckle.

146

The next day broke clear and sunny, promising a good day of fishing. We wolfed down our breakfast and got an early start. Firing up the skiff, Ezra headed west, speeding down the Middle Bight. The water was clear and shallow, underlain with coral and turtle grass. After covering our legs with sunblock, Steve and I sat back with our arms folded to enjoy the ride. The Middle Bight is a long, narrow cleft that divides Andros in half. During an hour of steady traveling, passing white sand beaches and green islets, we never saw a sign of human life.

Ezra finally slowed down, and we coasted into the white-sand shallows of an immense tidal flat. "Martha Stewart rods?" asked Steve.

I nodded. "Get up there and catch a bonefish."

Steve climbed on the casting platform, shook some line out of his fly rod, and got ready to meet his first bonefish. We scanned the water, whispering, as Ezra stealthily poled along. After ten minutes, a three-foot shark swam past, accompanied by its rakish shadow. Steve tossed a fly. The shark twisted in pursuit and engulfed his fly. Steve reared back on the rod and the leader snapped like a thread. We laughed. You need a wire leader to hook a shark, but it was fun to see it bite. Steve tied on another fly, and we carried on. Several days of high winds and driving rain had cooled the water down, and bonefish are sluggish feeders in a cold front. We hunted the flat all morning. We saw a couple of groups of bonefish, but they were skittish and didn't seem much interested in our offerings.

After lunch, I finally got a chance. A solitary bonefish came poking along, approaching us from behind. Ezra spun the boat around, and I prepared to cast, facing into what was gradually becoming a good afternoon breeze. Large bonefish generally gather in groups of three or four, and the biggest ones are often loners. This solitary fish was the biggest one I'd ever seen, and I could feel my nerves tightening as it came snuffling along the bottom toward us. I lofted a high back cast, letting the line straighten out, then drove the fly low into the headwind. More by fluke than anything, the line unfurled perfectly and the fly touched the water just a few feet away from the bonefish. I stripped once, twice, and the fish spotted the fly and swam toward it. "Let it sit," whispered Ezra. The bonefish inspected the fly, visibly shrugged, and turned away. My heart sank. It's discouraging to blow a chance like that, especially when you've been waiting all winter.

The tide was flooding in now, and more schools of bonefish were cruising past. Steve and I took turns throwing flies to them, but they weren't interested. Things were getting downright frustrating when Ezra suddenly hissed a warning and pointed his arm. We saw a huge black carpet on the sandy bottom. The dark shadow was perhaps a hundred feet wide, and it was gliding toward us. "What the hell is it?" I asked.

"Big school of bonefish," Ezra said.

Steve said, "Why are they so close together?"

The hundred-odd bonefish were so densely packed it was hard to pick out individuals. As the school approached, we saw the reason for their behavior. A number of large barracuda were escorting the school. As the bonefish turned, the barracuda turned, swimming alongside. It would have been easy for the barracuda to rush into the school and grab a bonefish, but as long as the fish stayed packed together the barracuda seemed reluctant to attack.

Steve flipped a fly toward the school. The bonefish ignored it, too frightened to think about food.

By the end of the day we'd covered sixty miles in that little open boat and caught nothing. Steve and I were a tired and sunburned pair as we boated back to the lodge. We'd seen quite a few fish that day—lots of barracudas, some nice jacks, three or four sharks, and plenty of bonefish—but none had fallen for our flies. Steve wasn't griping about our choice

Jacks or Better to Open

of tackle. But we would have caught something, probably, if we'd been using regular tackle, and I could hear him thinking it.

In the bar that night, a couple of stockbrokers from New York said they'd caught eight bonefish—distressing news. With a bit of questioning, they admitted they used bait— chunks of fresh conch meat on their flies. After they left, Steve suggested that we take some big spinning rods with us tomorrow and some hunks of bait.

"It's against the unwritten code."

"Fuck the code. Let's catch something."

I could see his point. We'd come all this way, and we still hadn't put a fish in the boat. The next morning, the bonefish were still sulking. We had no luck interesting them in our flies. Steve was beginning to seriously chafe under my Campaign of Moral Improvement. I think he was beginning to fantasize about lobbing a stick of dynamite at the next school of bonefish we encountered.

Midway through the morning, a big horse-eye jack swam past the boat. In silent rebellion, Steve had switched to a spinning rod, and when the jack swam past he flung a hunk of raw fish in its path. The jack pounced on the bait, and Steve's reel howled as the fish took off. Yes! The jack sped a hundred yards straight away, then darted sideways across the tidal flat. When a shark started chasing it, Ezra jumped in the water, galloping through the shallows toward the jack and slapping the water with his gaff to chase the shark away. It darted off, but the whole time Steve fought the jack the shark stayed in the area, gliding around and monitoring the proceedings. After a while the jack grew tired. Ezra walked slowly toward it, letting the line slide through his fingers. It was a big one, about fifteen pounds, and as Ezra hoisted it by the tail Steve let out a whoop. "That's more like it," Steve exclaimed, jumping in the water so that I could take his picture.

I aimed the camera. He was grinning like a kid. Then he handed me the fish. "Here, you ruby begonia. Pretend you caught it with your fly rod." I held up the big jack, with the fly rod in my hands. I was smiling into the camera and thinking, this is as low as it gets.

Ezra whacked the fish on the head and threw it in the boat. As we climbed into the skiff, Steve was eyeing the shark. It looked to be a decent-sized lemon shark, about a five-footer. He looked at Ezra. "Do you ever fish for those critters?"

"No sir."

"Why not?"

Ezra shrugged. "You need to use chum."

"What's chum?"

"You have to catch lots of small fish and scatter the pieces in the water."

"Can we try it?"

Ezra thought about it. "Yes sir, I believe we could."

Steve looked at me. "You want to try and catch that evil bastard?"

"I don't have the right rod."

Ezra said, "I could make some wire leaders for your fly rod."

It seemed a bit crude, using a wire leader and raw bait with my delicate Orvis fly rod, but I wasn't going to argue. "I guess we might as well. We're not doing very well with flies."

We motored out to a nearby reef and caught some little reef fish. Ezra tossed them in his bucket. When we had a dozen, we motored back to the tidal flat and anchored in the shallows. It was becoming hot and quiet, and the tide was flooding in over the white sand. Ezra cut up some of the

150

baitfish and tossed the pieces in the water. "We'll see if this attracts Mister Shark," he said. "They can smell it from a long way off."

Steve rigged up his spinning rod with a wire leader and a chunk of fish meat. I did the same with my fly rod. My rod looked so incongruous, rigged up that way, that Steve started laughing. On some outings, there's a moment when things become ridiculous. These are the moments that Steve lives for. He looked at Ezra. "Hey, Ez, you got any marijuana?"

Ezra chuckled. "No sir."

We waited for the shark and passed the time by drinking water and eating sandwiches. It was flat calm, white hot. I soaked my cotton neckerchief in the melted icewater at the bottom of Ezra's cooler and wrapped it around my neck. Man-of-war birds circled high overhead. Every few minutes, Ezra threw in another chunk of fish. Ten minutes passed, then fifteen. Sunlight flashed on the water. There wasn't a sign of life, and we didn't talk. Finally Ezra said, "There's a shark." A hundred yards away, a shadow was gliding toward us.

The shark cautiously circled the boat, staying just beyond casting range. Within minutes, it was joined by others. Soon we could count five or six sharks moving in wide, slow circles around the boat, all of them attracted by the molecules drifting away from these few small pieces of fish. Ezra pointed at one shark and said, "That's a big black-tip, almost six feet long."

They wouldn't come close enough to take our baits, so we slipped overboard and walked through the knee-deep water, carrying our baits in one hand and rods in the other. Most of the sharks shied away, but one smallish one, a three-footer, followed Ezra, attracted by the smell of fish. When it came within a few feet of him he slapped the water with his

151

gaff and it shied away. When we'd carried our baits a good distance from the boat, we dropped them in the water and walked back to the skiff.

It did not take long before the largest shark, the blacktip, approached one of the baits, picked it up off the bottom, and fled, chased by the others. I didn't know it was my bait until the line jumped to life in my hand. I tightened my fingers around the line and reared back on the rod. As soon as the shark felt the hook, something extraordinary happened. Just as one of those purring, docile-looking Japanese motorcycles can mutate into a screaming beast with a slight twist of the throttle, so did this docile shark morph into a different creature as soon as it tasted the hook. With a boil of water it took off at high speed, and the fly line shot through my fingers.

I tried to slow down the reel with my palm, but the howling spool burned my hand. I grabbed a glove, bunched it up and held it against the reel because I didn't have time to put it on. The reel's two hundred yards of backing was melting off quickly, so I pushed the glove harder against the reel and leaned back on the rod. At that point, the rod failed, right at the butt, snapping with a loud bang and spraying graphite splinters in my face. I hung onto the cork handle as the shark tore off the last few yards of line. When it hit the final knot, the line snapped.

I stood there with my expensive fly rod totally destroyed. Steve and Ezra were laughing. Then I started laughing too. Another rod bites the dust. What can you do?

Steve didn't waste any time trying to cheer me up. One of the sharks circled in and grabbed another piece of bait. Steve's reel suddenly whirred, and the shark was on. Steve struggled to keep the rod tip high, and the line tore off as the shark ran. Ezra got up on the casting platform and stood

beside him, slapping him on the back as he fought the shark.
"Good work, Steve," Ezra said.

I had to admit this was entertaining. I'd come here to teach
Steve about fly-fishing, and he was teaching me something
instead—that sometimes fishing is just about having fun.

Travels
WITH MY GIRL

◇◇◇◇◇

We saw our first alligator just a few miles outside Miami. It was a big one, and it was stalking some kids, edging toward them in the furtive manner of a thief, hoping that if it grabbed one of the boys and dragged him underwater nobody would notice.

It was a hot day in February. My daughter Caitlin and I were standing alongside the Florida highway talking to Grady Jackson, a seventy-eight-year-old black gentleman from Miami. He was sitting on the edge of a canal in a folding deck chair with a plastic cooler alongside him. The other members of his clan, perhaps a dozen men and women of various ages, were lined up alongside the canal. Like him, they were all using long bamboo fishing poles. Grady's baseball hat was tugged low on his sunglasses and he was watching the red-and-white slip bobber with the intent, slightly pathetic optimism of the dedicated fisherman. "I taught metal shops in a Miami high school all my life," he told us. "Now I'm old and I've got the cancer. But I don't think about that or anything else when I'm out here. I just enjoy the birds and the sunshine."

As we talked, his red-and-white bobber began bobbing. Grady snatched at his pole and hoisted a skinny, reptilian-looking creature from the water. "Walking catfish," he said with disgust. Pinning it to the grass with his boot, he pried the hook from its craw. "They're half fish, half beast. Once they eat all the fish in this canal, they'll climb up the hill and go walking across the highway."

Grady gave the fish a dismissive shove with his boot. It wriggled toward the water, wielding its fins with the clumsy motion of a snake experimenting with new elbows. Grady's perky eight-year-old grandsons, Brandon and Bryan, came running over to check out the catfish. As the boys squatted by the water's edge, I noticed something in the nearby marsh grass. It looked like a floating truck tire. I had to look at it closely, but it was definitely moving, pushing delicately through the reeds and drifting towards the boys.

Grady noticed the alligator. "There he is again," he said. "I've been watching that son of a gun all afternoon. Whenever the boys go down to the water, the 'gator tries to sneak over to them. He won't come up on the bank and grab me. He knows I'm too big. But he'll grab those kids if he gets a chance."

Grady climbed out of the deck chair. "Get away from the water," he said to the kids. "I must have told you a hundred times." He took a step toward the canal and waved his hat. The alligator stopped. The old man and the 65-million-year-old dinosaur stared at each other, a fishing pole's length apart. Grady picked up a stone. "Go on," he shouted. "Go on, you big son of a gun." He threw the stone at the alligator, and it disappeared in a swirl of muddy water.

Grady sat heavily in his chair and picked up his bamboo pole. "He'll be back," he said. "He's been confronting me all afternoon."

Caitlin smiled, not so much because she was enjoying this but because she knew I was pleased to see an alligator. I've always had a thing for the lower orders, particularly reptiles. When I was a kid I spent so much time reading about snakes and lizards that my parents assumed I would grow up to be a herpetologist. When I was about eight my parents gave my brother Danny and me a pair of pet turtles, two green red-eared sliders that we fussed over as if they were prize race-horses. The turtles came with their own enclosure, a plastic mini-environment with a water-filled moat and a tiny plas-tic palm tree. We dug up earthworms in the back yard and dropped them into the moat. Our turtles approached the worms with the same mix of hesitancy and determination dis-played by the alligator. They drifted up to the prey, cocked their heads to one side, scanned the target up and down for evidence of weaponry, then lunged, clamping their beaked jaws on the worms' midsections and tearing them to pieces with their claws. Sometimes the turtles escaped their plas-tic enclosure. We'd find them under our beds, looking glum, their bellies covered with lint.

As we grew older we graduated to bigger pets, wild tur-tles the size of saucepans, and I was seldom without a pet garter snake. The challenge in keeping snakes is building an escape-proof enclosure. Even now, in middle age, I can sel-dom look at a nice wooden butter box stacked in the rear of a grocery store without thinking *hmm, nice snake box*. Aquari-ums make practical snake enclosures, but I found them too cold and scientific. I wanted my snakes to have decent hous-ing, something I envisioned as a sort of miniature three-room apartment. In that profoundly half-assed way that kids do everything, I built a snake cage out of a wooden Coke crate, fitting it with a small bathtub, a dining area, and a partition separating the living quarters from the bedroom. The crate had slatted bottoms and grab holes in the side, and I wasn't a good enough carpenter to seal them properly. My snake would sometimes be AWOL for several weeks, and when it eventually turned up in the couch springs or one of their dresser drawers my sisters invariably flipped out, never considering the larger context.

The biggest creature in my reptile collection was a three-foot iguana named Socrates. He ran free in the house, did his mess on a sheet of newspaper, and perched high on the drapes above the living room window. Like many iguanas, Socrates got more aggressive as he grew larger, and eventually I was the only one who could handle him without risk of a good clawing. He was, I have to admit, a foul-tempered individual, and he ruined my secret plan to condition my parents and sisters to the idea of eventually acquiring a Florida alligator. My mother, who had already shown extraordinary forbearance in allowing me to have an escalating cast of reptiles, drew the line at an alligator. I appealed to my father, who never seemed to mind reading his evening newspaper with a lizard as long as his leg ensconced on the back of the couch. He backed my mother, pointing out that it was illegal to import alligators anyway. He said that when I grew up I could go down to Florida, where there were alligators all over the place. I've been to Florida at least a dozen times now. And every time I go, I never feel like I've really arrived until I spot my first 'gator.

After wishing Grady good luck with his fishing, Caitlin and I climbed back into our rental car. We were taking our annual father–daughter vacation. It's something that we've done ever since she was three years old, when her mother and I separated. Like a lot of men, I grew up thinking that household duty, including child care, was basically women's work, especially when the child was a girl rather than a boy. I believed that sons naturally relate to their fathers and daughters naturally relate to their moms.

Having a daughter changed all that. In the delivery room, the instant she was born, Caitlin looked right at me and smiled. I thought that babies cried when they were born. But she wasn't crying; she was grinning like an imp. When she was six months old she would bang her spoon on the high chair and chant, "da da da da da da!" when I walked into the room. When she was two years old, she devised a joke. There was a set of stairs leading down to the front door. As soon as she heard me come in the door, she would run toward the stairs and fling herself into space. I had to catch her, because here she came, ready or not.

By the time her mother and I separated, I'd come to realize that I much preferred having a daughter to having a son, especially this daughter. I also realized that if Caitlin and I were going to have a strong relationship, I would have to get serious about doing my share of the driving, the shopping, the doctor's appointments, and all the other myriad duties of raising children. There's an old saying, "A man who never becomes a father will always be a boy." In my case, at least, taking part in Caitlin's upbringing helped me to grow up. The rituals of fatherhood gave me a sense of weight I'd never felt before.

158   It was a twenty-minute drive to Montessori pre-school, through the wooded suburbs and along a river. We did the same drive for three years. Outside the car, the yellow leaves turned to falling snow, and the deep snows of winter melted in the heat of spring. Through the seasons, Caitlin and her

friend Erika sat in the back seat in their sunglasses, calling out requests for road tunes. Their favorite artist was Steve Earle, their favorite song "Sweet Little 66." When I parked the car and walked them into the old high school where the Montessori program was based, the photographs of the school's founding fathers stared at us from the wall. The names of the war dead, the graduating classes of the 1920s. They'd walked these halls too, and now they were gone.

Once school was out for the summer, Caitlin and I went to the lake. During the winter holidays we went to Mexico or the Bahamas or someplace else that was exotic and warm. I'd always wanted to show her the Everglades, so this year, to celebrate her sixteenth birthday, we'd come to Florida. We planned to spend a week just poking around. Usually we'd take turns planning the day's agenda. There are things I like to do, and things she likes to do. Girl things one day, guy things the next. We humor each other. Stopping to talk to Grady, for example, was for my benefit. Caitlin enjoyed seeing the walking catfish and the alligator, but we both knew she didn't enjoy them as much as I did.

As we drove on, the landscape on both sides of the highway was flat and endless. We were driving west on the Tamiami Trail, which is a narrow stretch of elevated two-lane blacktop running straight across the Everglades. This is not the Florida of plush condo developments and seaside hotels. The Glades are the largest undeveloped area in the lower forty-eight states, and apart from an occasional billboard advertising Seminole Indian airboat tours, the roadside was featureless. Caitlin is a movie buff. She's seen the movie *Adaptation,* where Meryl Streep tracks down the orchid thief in the woods of the Fakahatchee swamp, and when I told her we were in the Everglades she was surprised and perhaps a bit disappointed. Like most people, she expected mossy jungle. But most of the Everglades is as flat as Saskatchewan. The pioneers called it "the prairie," and that's what it looks like.

Even with the air conditioning, it was a hot day, and after an hour of driving Caitlin and I stopped at a ratty little roadside attraction (Authentic Indian Village!) and bought a couple of cold soda pops. We stood by the swamp and leaned against the railing, enjoying the feel of the sun's heat on our pale northern faces. Caitlin was wearing sunglasses and had her hair pinned back in a bun. As we drank our Cokes (hers the diet version, of course), we played Name That Species. Wetlands are the most fertile of all ecosystems, and this little place was thronging with life. In the shallow water of the marsh, a trio of prehistoric-looking garfish as thick as baseball bats floated indolently, stirring occasionally to nip at the clouds of minnows going by. Farther away, the water dimpled as smaller fish like bass and crappies sipped insects off the surface. The nearby undergrowth rustled as tiny lizards scampered about. On the far side of the marsh, coots, rails, gallinules, herons, egrets, and ibises poked along the shoreline. Overhead, buzzards and ospreys drifted on the high thermals. The whole place looked like one of those foldout pictorial illustrations in a nature book. I could have made a fatherly lesson of this, pointing out that the beauty of the Everglades resides in its detailing, but I kept quiet, letting Caitlin construct her own impressions. When I was around her age, I began to notice that nothing conforms to expectations. Faraway places always look different from what you imagined. It's confusing to find out you've been wrong, but the truths you acquire on a journey are more valuable than the illusions you lose.

We got back in the car and kept driving. We were heading for Everglades City, which is not a city but a forgotten sort

of village just off the Tamiami Trail. The turnoff is so incon-
spicuous that I missed it, and we had to wait for traffic to
thin out so that I could make a U-turn and double back. The
turnoff took us south along a narrow road, through palmetto
and cypress woods. Driving into the outskirts, we passed bait
shops and hand-painted alligator signs, then crossed a jungle river. In preparation for our trip I had studied up on the
history of the area, and I knew the founder of Everglades City
was an old-style buccaneer capitalist named Barron C. Collier. Collier named almost everything around here after himself—the Barron River, the local courthouse, and even this
part of the state (Collier County). As we drove through town,
Caitlin peered at the sun-bleached Spanish-style railroad station, the temple-columned Bank of the Everglades, and the
Everglades Rod & Gun Club, which is not a club but a white
clapboard hotel that looks like an old plantation house. She
was curious, because we planned to stay here for a week.

We hauled our bags into the hotel. Standing in the foyer,
we gazed around the dark, cool lobby. Off to one side was a
massive-legged wooden billiard table. The cypress walls were
hung with alligator skins, antique wooden clocks, old maps,
bear hides, turn-of-the century rifles, and dusty trophy tarpon. Ceiling fans rotated lazily overhead, and Glenn Miller's
Air Force Band played from the dining room.

I knew the hotel was an offbeat place when I phoned
to make a reservation and the manager told me they didn't
accept credit cards. All hotel bills had to be paid in cash,
and at the front desk there was no sign of a computer or fax
machine. The stone-faced desk clerk rang my deposit into
an old nickel-plated cash register. He said there was only
one phone in the whole hotel, and it was the rotary-dialed
bakelite phone right in front of us. Caitlin and I, both phone

addicts, exchanged silent looks of dismay. It looked as if we would be going into withdrawal for a while. I assumed this eccentric approach to hotel management was marketing shtick, the idea being to make you feel as if you'd stepped through a hole in the Twilight Zone and somehow landed in the Florida of the 1940s. But as the week passed, it became apparent that there was nothing calculated about it. The entire town was a leafy museum of antiquated conservative values. Most of the locals we met seemed to honestly believe that the world would be a better place if the past half-century had never happened.

Caitlin and I checked into our cabin. It had twin beds and a nice veranda overlooking the Barron River. We chose beds, unpacked our bags, and took turns changing into bathing suits to go for a swim. Carrying towels, we walked gingerly across the spiky grass in our tender bare feet. The pool was empty. I waded in, enjoying the bite of the cool water, and floated on my back, watching Caitlin as she stood on the edge and stiffened for a shallow dive. She swims well enough to qualify as a lifeguard, but when she was young she was terrified of water. Her mother and I took her to swimming lessons downtown. It was midwinter and bitterly cold. Even though her lessons took place right after school, it would be dark by the time we got to the pool. Walking along the icy sidewalk, you could smell chlorine on the wind from half a block away. I felt like a cruel parent, making Caitlin go swimming on a night like this, and even after a winter of lessons she was convinced that only a "freak" would jump into deep water. That summer at the lake, I'd treaded water for five minutes, pleading with Caitlin to join me. Clinging to the swimming ladder, her life jacket buckled to her chin and her stick-thin arms shivering in the wind, she'd howl that I was trying to kill her. Then without warning she'd leap, land on top of my head and cling like a monkey. After two months of doing this it finally occurred to Caitlin that swimming was fun. She and her friends would spend the entire day in the water, beseeching me to serve as a judge in their never-ending inquiry into who among them could fling herself into the lake in the most demented fashion.

Now, entering the water like a knife, Caitlin surfaced smoothly and swam laps for a few minutes without stopping. Then she floated on her back, looking up at the fluffy clouds. Climbing out, we moved a couple of chaise longues into the partial shade of some high palm trees and relaxed for a while in the afternoon heat. For some reason my passport was in the pocket of my bathing suit. After examining its sodden pages, I laid it out beside me to dry in the sun. I tend to be a corner-cutter when it comes to travel, believing in the old fallacy that all you really need is your toothbrush and a credit card. I'm an Aries, which according to Zena the Star Woman means I'm the sort of person who'd rather hit the road with crossed fingers than do a lot of planning. This is the most charitable interpretation, the other being that I'm simply a fuckup.

On this particular trip I'd promised Caitlin that we'd rent a convertible. Through my travel agent I got a cheap rate on a Sebring for the week, but when we got to Miami airport I realized I'd left the reservation back home in my drawer. I couldn't remember the name of the rental company, so I had to do a walk-in at the Alamo office and rent a crappy little Neon that ended up costing three times as much. This is a typical performance of mine, I'm afraid. When Caitlin was eight, I agreed to take her to Disney World in Orlando. We showed up at the airport at five in the morning. She had been packed for days, was carrying her rag doll and sunglasses. I

163

had a letter of permission from Caitlin's mother, but I'd forgotten to bring the original copy of her birth certificate—
without it, we were going nowhere. Her mom saved the day,
showing up at the last minute in her nurse's uniform with the
proper documents.

That evening, we ate an excellent dinner of grouper and
rice in the veranda. In Everglades City, the main entertain-
ment is the sunset. Florida weather is such that, in the late
afternoon, thunderheads tend to pile up over the Gulf of
Mexico. By evening, the sun is burning down through the
clouds and the distant clouds look like great hulking galle-
ons, illuminated from within by occasional flashes of lightning. After it got dark, Caitlin and I went into the lounge to
play some billiards. Between shots, we looked at the framed
photographs and old newspaper pages that documented the
early history of Everglades City.

According to the pictorial evidence, the town's beloved
founder, Barron Collier, had made a fortune up north, mount-
ing advertisements on streetcars. Traveling in his gleaming
brass and mahogany steamboat the *Barroness*, named after
his wife, Collier arrived here in 1921. His modest plan was
to build a great metropolis, but inconveniently, most of his
new land was either soggy marshland or coastal mangrove
forest, subject to tidal submersion and periodic flooding. Like
any good capitalist, Collier wasn't about to let Mother Nature
foil his dreams. He brought in floating suction dredges, huge
machines that spewed the reeking mud onto the surrounding
riverbanks, where bulldozers flattened it out in the shape of
a townsite. As the new community grew, Collier made sure
that he owned everything: the bakery, the hotel, the movie
theater, the liquor store, and the bank. He owned the Juliet
C. Collier Hospital, and he owned the doctors and nurses

who worked there. He built a trolley car line to move people back and forth. The steam whistle he mounted in the center of town blew every morning to wake people up, blew at noon to send them home for lunch, and blew again at 12:55 to summon them back to work. Collier was the driving force behind the campaign to build the Tamiami Trail, and when the highway was completed in 1928 the price of Everglades swampland shot up to ninety-two dollars per acre. Encouraged by Collier's example, other land speculators bought up great packages of swamp. They encouraged aspiring settlers to get in on the ground floor of the land boom.

But on September 16, 1928, an enormous hurricane blew in from the Atlantic and swept across southern Florida. It was a wet year, and water levels in the Glades were already high. The highest point of land along the Tamiami Trail is only twelve feet above sea level. Like most hurricanes, this one pushed a storm surge ahead of it—a bulge of tidal water that, depending on factors like time of day and phase of the moon, can rise to eighteen feet above sea level. The farmers who had purchased "farmland" from Collier knew little of the coming danger. There was no weather forecasting then, no telephones to warn little Everglades communities like Belle Glade, Pahokee, or Chosen. When the surge came rolling across the Glades like some visitation straight out of the Old Testament, residents tried to take shelter on their rooftops and barns, but buildings were torn apart by 150-mile-per-hour winds. In all, 1,800 people died. It was the second-worst storm death toll in American history. One year later, the arrival of the Great Depression delivered the coup de grâce to Collier's Ozymandian dream. Everglades City, which was supposed to become the biggest city in the southern United States, now has a year-round population of about three hundred.

165

When Caitlin and I took a walk through town after our game of billiards, there wasn't a sign of life. We found a public phone attached to a pole across from the Bank of the Everglades. Caitlin checked in with her mom, and I sat on a bench a little ways off to give her some privacy. It was still hot and muggy, even though it was midwinter and getting onto eleven o'clock at night. An occasional mosquito buzzed about my head as I sat watching the moths twirl around the streetlights. A pickup truck rumbled by with two mullet-haired rebel boys inside. One of them said something to Caitlin as they idled past. She ignored them, as I suppose young women must learn to do, but I had the normal fatherly temptation to shout a reply.

There's always a hint of menace in these quiet Florida towns. When you flip through the local newspaper, you don't have to look too hard to find it. I'd seen an item earlier that day about the discovery of a woman's dismembered body in a campground not far from here. A while ago, a convict had escaped from the Everglades Correctional Facility in a stolen car. When a highway patrolman stopped him, the convict managed to take away his gun. While a group of horrified motorists watched, the convict made the cop kneel down and beg, then shot him in the head. I would never let Caitlin come out here in the darkness and make these phone calls alone.

The first time we came to Florida, for the aforementioned trip to Disney World, I explained to Caitlin that she was, so to speak, no longer in Kansas. "This is Florida," I said. "You see all these cars going by? If you stopped them and looked inside, you'd find that quite a few have a loaded pistol in the glove compartment. People carry guns for self-defense. This looks like home, but it's not like home. There are a lot of bad people here."

She was in the back seat, holding an *Archie* comic. I could see her eyes in the rearview mirror. She was nodding, listening.

"So if you get lost, or get separated from your poppa for any reason, go and find a nice-looking lady. Don't tell a man. Find a lady who looks like your mom or your grandma and tell her, and she'll help you, okay?"

It had been a long day's journey, flying down to Orlando, and I couldn't find the hotel. Finally we got checked in and hauled our bags up the stairs. Caitlin was hungry and homesick. I gave her a block of cheese and my Swiss Army knife. She tried to cut the cheese but pressed her thumb against the wrong side of the blade, and I heard a wail. Blood poured from her thumb. Calmly, I made her lie down and hold her arm aloft. Then I called the front desk and told them my daughter had cut herself. Would they please send up a medical kit? A few minutes later the phone rang. The guy on the line identified himself as hotel security. "What exactly is going on up there?"

It was late in the evening. We hadn't eaten yet, and after going through customs and security checks all day I didn't need any more questions from petty officialdom. "Listen, bud, it's none of your business. Just send up the Band-Aids, alright?"

A few minutes later there was a knock on the door. I opened it, but there was no one there. I peered around the corner and saw a gray-haired guy with his back pressed against the wall and his hand on his hip. He said, "Step away from the door and keep your hands where I can see them."

I couldn't help smiling. "You're kidding."

"Sir, I was a police officer in Queens for twenty-five years. I don't kid."

"Did you bring the Band-Aids?"

"Step away from the door," he repeated. He peered inside. "What happened, honey?"

Caitlin explained what happened.

The guy grudgingly handed me the Band-Aids.

I went inside and bandaged her thumb. I thought, yep, we're definitely in Florida. A few minutes later the phone rang again. It was the front desk, telling me I'd left my head-lights on. Caitlin was in her pajamas by now. She was afraid to stay in the room alone, so we went down to the parking lot together. It was dark. I walked toward the medium-sized sil-ver car, discernible among the dozens of other medium-sized silver cars by the gleam of its headlights. I opened the door, shut off the lights, and turned around. Caitlin was nowhere in sight.

I walked between the rows, expecting to spot her. But she was gone. With a rising feeling of dread I searched the park-ing lot. At that moment my friend the ex-cop appeared. He gave me a suspicious look. "Having a problem?"

"No," I snapped.

I walked toward the hotel lobby. No sign of Caitlin. Back toward the pool area. This was bad, very bad. As I scaled the stairs toward our room, I heard someone coming down. It was a lady, saying, "We'll find your daddy, don't worry." She rounded the corner and I saw Caitlin. They were holding hands, and they were both crying. I thanked the woman profusely. Cait-lin told me she had gone around one side of a parked truck. I had gone around the other. When she couldn't see me, she panicked and ran back to the hotel. For the rest of the week, whenever we saw the nice lady by the pool we waved.

The Rod and Gun Club was dark and deserted when we returned from the public telephone. Crickets were chirping in the grass, and the Barron River glistened in the moonlight.

Our plan was to go fishing the next day. Fishing is something that Caitlin enjoys doing, so we hadn't had to flip a coin to see who was in charge of planning the day. Our fishing guide was Captain Brian Richardson, who grew up in Everglades City and spends most of his time squiring sports fishermen from all over the world in pursuit of snook, tarpon, and sea trout. We met him at the dock in front of the club, packed some sandwiches and drinks into his boat, and headed off to explore the coastal Everglades. As we cruised away from the dock, a huge animal rolled out of the water right in front of us, blowing off air with a pneumatic hiss and lifting its paddled tail to dive. "What the heck is that?" Caitlin exclaimed.

"Manatee," said Captain Brian. "We have to run the boats real slowly through here or we'll hit them. They're everywhere."

"What do they look like?"

"You ever see a walrus? Just like that, except they don't have tusks."

A mile beyond the Rod and Gun Club, the Barron River opened up into a wide bay. The water was as bright as a tin sheet in the morning sun, and just ahead of us an osprey dropped like a broken kite into the calm water, emerging with a mullet in its claws. No sooner did the osprey gain altitude than a bald eagle came laboring across the bay, intent on strong-arming the fish from the osprey.

We cruised up the right side of the bay and turned into a mangrove creek, a meandering waterway entirely obscured by foliage. The sun came down through the interlaced leaves and dappled the green water with sunlight. In some places, the branches were so low we had to duck. Captain Brian told us that Richard Nixon had come fishing in this same creek. He had gotten hit by branches and fallen out of the

169

boat, twice. Unfortunately there was no tape recorder running at the time.

Tidal current whirled past submerged logs. We could see small fish holding in the current, darting away from the looming shadow of the boat. "Lots of snook here," Brian observed. "They hold in these little shadowy pockets along the edge of the creek and ambush baitfish as they go by."

Mangroves make a transition zone between the freshwater Everglades and the saltwater estuaries of the Gulf of Mexico. The small white-tailed deer that live here are hunted by the Florida panther. "I've lived here all my life, but I've only seen panthers half a dozen times," said Captain Brian. Several miles up the mangrove creek, a big porpoise appeared out of nowhere. Heading straight over to the boat, it circled us for several minutes, blowing, cavorting, and rubbing against the prow.

After fishing unsuccessfully in the mangrove forests for a few hours, we made our way back out to the bay. Captain Brian fed the big Yamaha some gas, and we felt a welcome breeze on our faces as we sped past islands, white-sand beaches, and channel markers topped with ragged osprey nests. This area is called the Ten Thousand Islands. It looked like backwoods Canada, except the islands were clad with tropical trees instead of evergreen scrub, and a disturbance in the calm water ahead meant a big leopard ray had broken the surface, or perhaps a tarpon or sea turtle.

When we stopped and cast lures for sea trout, Caitlin caught one. She often catches more fish than I do. She has what fishing guides call the "the touch." I first noticed this when she was about nine. Caitlin and I were visiting Vancouver, and one day we cruised out in a rented boat toward Bowen Island, surrounded by those preposterously brawny

170

coastal mountains. I fished for two or three hours with nary a bite. We only had one rod, and I didn't give it to Caitlin because I didn't know at the time that she was a child savant. Finally, as I was preparing to admit defeat, Caitlin opened the little tackle box and said, "Why don't we try this one?"

The lure she'd chosen, a frog-spotted bass plug, was the most inappropriate lure in the box. But our fishing trip was a bust anyway, so I clipped the lure onto the line and handed her the rod. In a minute or two she had caught a salmon. She reeled it in, we took a picture, and I let it go. A few minutes later, she caught another one. When I was a young fishing guide, I used to see this happen all the time. The middle-aged male client would show up at the boat with his wife, who had never fished before. Out on the water, his self-respect would gradually crumble as his wife innocently caught one fish after another while he caught nothing.

After Caitlin had established that her mojo was still working, Captain Brian beached the boat at Sandfly Key, a breezy, pleasant island with a deserted sandy beach. It's hard to believe, but about one hundred islands along this coast, including this one, were built centuries ago by the Calusa Indians, who hauled boatloads of shells to choice locations and used a combination of shells and marl to make canals, dikes, and defensive moats. Sandfly Key is seventy-five acres in size, which makes it one of the largest shell islands in the Everglades. Captain Brian pointed out a big pond in the center of the key, like a hole in a doughnut. The Indians had built it as a self-operating fish trap. At high tide, fish would swim into the pond. As the tide went out, the Calusas would stretch a net across the opening, trapping the fish.

On our second day in Everglades City, it was Caitlin's turn to set the agenda, so we headed for the beaches of Naples. As we drove west along the highway, the marshlands shimmering in the heat, I told Caitlin about the poor saps who'd had to build this road. The Tamiami Trail was Barron Collier's idea, but he didn't get involved in the actual work. That was left to the immigrant workers, who had to cope with the heat, the bugs, and the "sawgrass," a ubiquitous Everglades tall grass that looks innocent enough but, in close contact, lacerates human flesh like razor wire. Struggling forward through knee-deep muck, the first wave of construction workers had to clear the sawgrass by hand. Underneath the thickets of sawgrass were layers of water, muck, and jagged limestone. This limestone is studded with absurdly vicious hooks and prongs. It's not only sharp but poisonous, and it causes nasty infections with even a small puncture wound. The plan was to blast the limestone and fill the roadway with crushed rock, but muck kept pouring back into the excavation. The construction site became a treacherous hell of tangled logs, sharp rocks, roaring dredges, and clouds of mosquitoes "so thick," swore one worker, "you could scoop them off your neck in handfuls." The laborers were dismembered by machinery, bitten by poisonous snakes, drowned, crushed, and blown to pieces by faulty charges of dynamite. The job was supposed to take two years, but it took twelve. Collier and his partners never bothered to keep track of how many men were killed during the project.

In Naples, Caitlin and I parked our car and wandered through the town. Naples is one of those extremely wealthy American enclaves where the gleaming cars, the palatial homes, and even the spotless patio-stone roadways look as if they are given a good vacuuming by a team of Filipino maids every morning. We stopped for lunch at a wharf district called Tin City and watched the immense white yachts rumble past.

We didn't make small talk. One of the nice things about traveling with your daughter is getting to that level where silence
is comfortable. Caitlin tends to be an inward sort of person
anyway. Her family is Scottish and Irish on both sides, and she
leans toward West Highlands taciturnity. She'll always tell you
her opinion if you ask for it, but if you want to find out how she
feels you have to listen closely. Even when it's against her inter-
ests, she'll err on the side of saying nothing. For example, after
lunch, while I nursed a beer and studied the boats, she told
me she wanted to walk across the street and look at a clothing
store. When she came back, we had our normal shopping conversation, which usually goes something like this.

"Hi, honey, did you find anything?"

"Nope."

"Nothing you liked?"

"Nope. Well . . . I saw one really nice shirt."

"They didn't have your size?"

"They did, but it was too much money."

"How much?"

"Twenty-four dollars."

"How much do you have?"

"Nineteen."

"Do you want five dollars?"

"That's all right, Dad, you don't have to do that."

"Don't be silly." I took out my wallet and gave her the five
dollars.

She kissed my cheek and skipped off to buy the shirt.
Some people might point out that she plays me like a fiddle,
which I suppose is true. But all kids ask for money, and this
is how she does it. If we didn't spend so much time together,
I might not understand that "Nope" actually means "Can I
have five dollars?"

After she'd bought her shirt Caitlin and I walked down to the main pier, where hundreds of people strolled in the sun. At the very end of the pier, a motley crew of fishermen was gathered. One of them was hooked up to a large fish. He was struggling with it, his big spinning rod bent in a fierce arc. Every public pier in America seems to have a group like this, ex-soldiers and bikers, guys with dark tans, lawnmower haircuts, and tattoos on their muscular arms. These guys had shopping carts stuffed with fishing tackle, bait, and sleeping bags. One of them told me he'd been out here for two days, sleeping on the deck and getting by on hot dogs and beach-vendor pretzels. "Here it comes," he said, pointing toward the waves. "Nice little hammerhead."

The shark didn't look little to me. It was at least seven feet long, much bigger than the guy who was hauling it in. It rolled and thrashed on the surface, twisting against the wire leader. Caitlin and I leaned against the rail, our shoulders pressed together by the crowd of people around us. Everyone wanted to see the shark. On the nearby beach, swimmers were standing hip-deep in the waves and clapping as the boys lowered a gaff hook. As the shark thrashed in the waves right below us, the guy beside me yanked the line and set the gaff hook in the shark's gills. Then he reefed the line around a timber. "We'll pull it up after it gets dark."

"You're going to just leave it there?" Caitlin asked. The shark was twisting on the hook. Every time a wave rolled in it turned upside down, revealing its white underbelly. Its mouth looked like the tragic frown on an actor's mask.

174

"It's illegal to catch sharks off the pier," the guy said. "If we bring it up now somebody will take a picture and we might get charged."

"Why is it illegal?"

He shrugged. "This city councillor came out here, and we asked him the same question. He said, 'You can't fish for sharks because there aren't any.' I guess they think sharks are bad for tourism."

"What will you do with it?" I asked.

The guy who'd caught it produced a cigarette. "Chop it up and barbecue it," he said, lighting the smoke with a dismissive snap. "Sharks don't eat us. We eat them."

Caitlin and I headed back to the car. It was getting late and we were ready to go home, which by now was how we were thinking of our little cabin in Everglades City. On the way out of Naples we stopped at a convenience store, and Caitlin bought some bottled water so she could take her pills. Three times a day, at regular intervals, she goes through this routine. It all started a few years ago, when we were on the Caribbean island of Nevis. One rainy afternoon she came to me with a worried look. "I was playing cards with Lexanne and I dropped my cards on the floor. It's like my brain went blank."

She looked afraid.

I told her it was probably nothing, but I too was worried. As soon as we got home I talked to her mother, and we scheduled a doctor's appointment. Caitlin's doctor referred her to a neurologist, who recommended a number of tests, including a sleep-deprivation EEG. She had to take the test while she was very tired, so we stayed up all night. We rented movies, played cards, and went to the 7-Eleven at four in the morning. Caitlin was worried that she had a brain tumor, and the doctor declined to rule out that possibility. With the drinks we'd bought at the 7-Eleven, we walked along the river. It wasn't quite dawn, but the sky was getting light. I felt privileged to weather this long night with her.

She took the tests and the results came back: no brain tumor, but low-grade epilepsy. The doctor told Caitlin she could take medication and stave off the possibility of a major seizure, or she could bide her time and hope she'd grow out of it. Being a fitness buff, she didn't want to take medication. That worked fine for a while. But one morning her friend Erin called me, shrieking in terror. I rushed over to Caitlin's mother's house to find a scene of utter chaos. Caitlin's hair was a mess, her tongue was bleeding, and she was unable to stand up. She was crying in bewilderment. "What's happening to me?"

After I called an ambulance, we spent the day in the hospital. Over the next two weeks Caitlin had two more grand mal attacks, one of which dislocated her shoulder. She began taking medication, which controlled the seizures, but I still worry about it. I worry when she has a bath and I worry when she goes to the lake for the weekend. I guess that's what parents do, worry. But she's learned from Nietzche: "Dad, if it doesn't kill me, it makes me stronger," and I know she's right. This tribulation will help forge her into the strong woman she is going to become.

That night, back in our messy cabin, we ate pizza and watched stupid American TV, surely one of life's great uncelebrated pleasures. The trip was falling into a rhythm. We had no ambitions except taking it easy, surrendering to the hedonism that seems unimaginable when you're living your normal life—chasing the clock and fighting rush-hour traffic. Next day we took a boat ride again, this time to check out a place that I thought Caitlin and I might rent one day. It was a "chickee," which in the Everglades is what they call a cabin in the woods. This one was a crooked old shack on a sandy beach, built on spindly stilts to raise it above high tide and the occasional hurricane surge.

After poking around the shack, which you could rent from the park service for ten dollars a night, Caitlin and I sat on a bench in the shade of the front porch. We unpacked some chicken sandwiches and cold drinks from our cooler. The shack looked out toward the open sea. The water was flat calm in the noon heat.

We sat quietly eating our lunch, looking out at the water. In a remote part of my brain, I knew that in our home town it was winter. At this moment, snow was probably falling on the gothic rooftops of our city. The kids in Caitlin's class were probably bent over their desks, scratching away with their pens. The phone in my office was probably ringing off the hook. Before long, Caitlin and I would drop back into our schedules. Our lives would once again be dictated by duty and commitments.

She was growing up, and the day would come when we would no longer take these trips together. She'd be traveling with her husband or with her own kids. That was the way of the world. But right now, as we sipped our drinks in the shade, worries of work and time's passing seemed very far away.

Once Again,
OLD FRIENDS

◇◇◇◇◇

There are about two dozen members of our hunting group, and over the years everyone has scattered to the four winds. Kerry Dennehy lives in Whistler. Skinner Wilson lives in Calgary. Chopper Macdonald lives in Collingwood, and Dwight Brainerd lives in the Queen Charlottes. But we stay in touch, and every October we meet for a week of waterfowl hunting in western Manitoba.

We used to go to a different part of the province every year, perennially searching for the ultimate place, an idyllic prairie town with nice accommodation, good home cooking, rolling countryside, lots of lakes and sloughs, and ducks galore. The trouble is, that describes just about every farm town on the Prairies. After auditioning a dozen or more towns, we finally settled on Binscarth. Driving into Binscarth is like entering a short story by W.O. Mitchell: the big dusty elms, the old pickup trucks, the preposterously wide and deserted streets, the half-dozen or so humble storefronts—coffee shop, hardware store, feed store, grain elevator, Chinese restaurant (there's one in every town along the rail line), and the Texaco station with its antique gas pumps and its fat, crippled collie dog who walks around with a sprig of hay protruding from his mouth. We stay at the town's only hotel—the "580"—a two-story wood-frame building with a restaurant, a dark wood-paneled beer parlor, and a warren of rooms upstairs.

You check in by hauling your stuff upstairs and claiming any room that doesn't have clothes and shotguns piled on the bed. You can walk in and out of all the rooms, because you're in a part of the country where nobody uses keys. You don't need to lock your guns up, either, because government theories about gun crime have no relevance here. You could walk into the coffee shop in your camouflage duds, break open your pumpgun, lean it in the corner and nobody would bat an eye. There are guns everywhere, but there's no crime. The last time anyone saw an RCMP cruiser was a few months ago, when the cops came through town to solicit sponsorships for their annual Torch Run.

We stay for a full week, and some of the bigger rooms can become as boisterous as fraternity parties after the big homecoming game. So I like to stay in one of the single rooms at the far end of the hall. It doesn't matter which room you choose, because they're all outfitted with the same lurid multicolored carpeting, small bathroom, and miniature black-and-white television with two fuzzy channels.

After dropping my bags on the narrow bed, I head downstairs to the dining room to join the rest of the boys. A room here is twenty-five dollars a night, and the meals, too, are what you could safely call "affordable." Reading the menu posted on the dining room door gives you the feeling that you've dropped through a hole in the space–time continuum and landed in 1956. Since we more or less take over the hotel during our stay, the women in the kitchen prepare a nightly feast and charge us by the head. Tonight, it seems we're having home-cooked turkey, mashed potatoes, and corn on the cob, accompanied by real pumpkin pie and whipped cream, all of which will probably set us back about eight bucks each.

We sit at tables arranged in a long row, and there are great rounds of cheers and catcalls as newcomers enter the room. Handshakes and high fives go up and down the line. We've known each other all our lives, but nowadays we usually only see each other once a year. Most of us grew up in Winnipeg, where we went to school and played hockey and learned to hunt under the tutelage of our fathers, skipping school on autumn Fridays and going off to hunt ducks on the big marshes of Lake Winnipeg and Lake Manitoba. We weren't allowed to carry guns at first, but when we got a little older we learned to shoot, and like most quick-handed, sharp-eyed teenagers we were pretty good at it. I couldn't understand how anyone could miss a flying duck. (I'm an expert at missing them now.) And most of my friends could shoot better than I could. Victor Mann was like a robotic duck-shooting machine. And Paul Sweatman was hell on wheels with his little 20-gauge automatic. But no matter how well we shot, the old boys weren't impressed. To them, the object wasn't to shoot well, but to hunt well. The object was to be humble, try hard, stay keen, use your creativity, be generous to others, pull your share of the load, and muster graciousness in the face of disappointment. To them, the skills that went into producing a good hunt were the same skills required to produce a good life. Their attempts at teaching us those skills must have succeeded, because they're gone but we're still here.

With the excitement of being back in our old haunt, we adjourn to the bar after dinner. It's usually quiet on weekday nights, so it's like having our own party room. The walls are adorned with the heads of immense whitetail bucks, and the jukebox is full of songs we haven't heard since we were in high school. The passing hours are marked by the crack of pool balls and the thunder of the jukebox.

When we were younger, these evenings would sometimes get a little out of control. Once the beer started to flow, our sojourn in the bar would turn into an all-nighter, with enough side-plots going on to fill a two-hour episode of the *Dukes of Hazzard*. We used to stay, for example, at a very pleasant town called Glenboro. But one night Jimmy White and a few of the other boys ate some magic mushrooms and staged a loud sporting event on the main street in front of the hotel. Whitey is a gentle character. He brings his gun on our hunting trips, but I'm not sure he ever loads it. He is soft-spoken and philosophical and intensely curious about ethics and other matters that most people never think about. But if you give Whitey a drink, no, two drinks, his eyes start to burn with a mad glitter that brings to mind those daguerreotype photographs of John Brown after he was captured in the raid on Harper's Ferry.

The second night of our hunting trip is when Whitey normally goes a bit wild. He makes his rounds while everyone else is sleeping, plunking himself down on the edge of someone's bed at four in the morning and insistently asking, "So what do you want to talk about now?" That particular year in Glenboro we arrived during Indian summer, warm enough to be outside in a T-shirt even in the middle of the night, which was when Whitey and some of the other guys staged the spirited touch football game that lasted all night and got us expelled from the hotel.

The next town we tried didn't work out either. LaRiviere is a pretty little village set in the bottom of a deep wooded valley. If Duddy Kravitz saw LaRiviere, he'd say, "Wow, I love this town. How much does this town cost?" For a couple of seasons it looked as if LaRiviere was going to be a perfect base of operations. But one night after the bar closed, Steve Alsip and I decided to go skunk hunting. It's a well-known fact that skunks prey on lesser creatures, like baby rabbits, so we planned to strike a blow for rabbitdom. After taping flashlights to our gun barrels and mixing up a thermos of rum and Coke, we sallied forth, cruising through the bottomlands in Steve's old car. We spotted a skunk waddling down the road toward us. But it seemed to know that we bore it malice, because it scuttled out of sight as soon as we hit the brakes. As we continued through the pasture, Steve's headlights illuminated a strange sight. Right in front of us, a huge Hereford bull was mating with a heifer. It was full uncensored hot bull-on-cow action. Getting into the spirit of the encounter, Steve eased the grill of his old Pontiac up behind the bull and started prodding it in the rump, adding extra momentum to its labours. Suddenly our doors opened and we discovered ourselves surrounded by three burly, irate ranchers. It turned out they were manning an all-night ambush for the rustlers who had been stealing their cattle, and we had blundered into it.

We were carrying incriminating evidence, like guns with flashlights taped to their barrels, and the ranchers acted as if they were considering hanging us on the spot. We were young and clearly untrustworthy, and Steve's 1961 Laurentian had a bent coat hanger for an aerial. So they didn't believe Steve when he insisted he was a lawyer. But as we stood there in the glare of the headlights Steve delivered a sweep-

182

ing, impassioned legal condemnation of skunks that would have made any lawyer proud.

The farmers weren't totally convinced, but Steve introduced enough doubt that they released us, with the caution that they were going to convey our license number and names to the RCMP. That pretty much ruined our reputations in LaRiviere. We moved on, like a convoy of boll weevils. We tried a new town every hunting season, and each one brought a new set of problems. We moved from Wawanesa to Redvers to Rorketon, leaving a trail of bad karma behind us. Hunters are always working to clean up their image in the public eye, and we weren't helping. I'd like to say that we learned our lesson by the time we discovered Binscarth, but the problem wasn't solved by us getting wiser, just older.

Nowadays we're usually in bed by midnight. My room is at the upper corner of the hotel, and when I'm in bed with the lights off it feels as if I'm lying in the forward berth of an old ship, pushing forward into the night. In western Manitoba it seems that the wind never stops blowing. The windows are drafty, so it's pleasantly cool in the room. Sometimes I wake up in the middle of the night and check my watch, but it's always still hours until morning. It's deliciously comfortable to lie here in the darkness, listening to the muttering of the wind and sometimes, high overhead, far above this hotel and this little town, the faint bark of migrating geese.

The first thing you hear in the morning is the thumping of boots and the flushing of toilets. Paul Craft comes walking down the hallway, knocking on doors. Paul is also known *183* as Wheatso, the Indian, Gator, and various other nicknames. Everyone has a variety of these nicknames, and they're used without thought; if this were a convention we'd all be wearing half a dozen name tags. Paul is our unofficial huntmeister, and he'd remind us of our mommy if he didn't remind us so much of our dad. After getting dressed, grabbing a quick feed of bacon and eggs in the coffee shop and filling our thermoses, we head out into the darkness of the parking lot, where the trucks are rumbling in the cold.

It's hard to hunt effectively in a large group, so we split up into small teams. One of the rules of duck hunting is that you're always running behind schedule. By the time we've loaded up the trucks, covered twenty miles of gravel road, arrived at our secret grain field, unloaded the truck, and climbed into our heavy clothes, there's already a smear of pink in the eastern sky.

While we plant our five or six dozen duck decoys in the stubble field, there's usually a testy debate about the proper configuration of the setup. Our hunting group is long on chiefs and short on Indians. As we hurry around in the darkness, Peter Dickson and John Kilgour get into a ritualized conversation that goes something like this:

"John, you're putting these birds too close together."

"Peter? Fuck off."

After deploying the decoys we set up our blinds, using netting that looks like a blend of fallen leaves and wheat straw. Finally we get settled on both sides of the decoys. The stars are still out, and a comic-book moon hangs in a corner of the sky. We blow experimentally on duck calls, load our guns, and organize some loose shells into a handy coat pocket. We uncap our thermoses and pour hot cups of coffee. I take a sip and balance my cup on the ammunition box beside me, where it steams in the cold. I habitually check my safety and scan the horizon.

When I was a kid I'd be vibrating with adrenaline by this point. I'd be staring holes in the landscape, trying to use sheer mind control to make some lone mallard come winging out of the gloom, headed right toward me. I wanted to make the gun kick and roar, and make the duck tumble. Nowadays, I'm not much worried about whether the birds will come. Mother Nature no longer owes me anything. It's sufficient just to be here, to watch the eastern sky begin to glow, and to exchange some whispered banter with old friends.

We hunt in different groups every morning. It gives you a chance to get updated on everyone's personal life. Some of the news is good, some not so good. As Hank Williams put it, we'll never get out of this world alive. Talking to your old buddies is sometimes like listening to dispatches from the war. Marriages have broken down, and several of the boys have lost their jobs in the economic downturn. Some members of the group have lost their sons to suicide. After we've ingested the news, the fact that we're all still here seems like even more of a privilege. The early morning marsh, the bright stars, the yip of distant coyotes, the pink sunrise, the rattle of the wind in the bulrushes—these things existed long before we did, and they'll be here long after we're gone. Coming here every year, hunting together, is one of the ways we connect to the abiding earth.

When the morning hunt is over, we spend the day jump-shooting. The hills of western Manitoba are pocked with abandoned farms. Almost every time you top a hill you see another one just ahead—a wooded windbreak, rusty machines overgrown with weeds, and a grizzled old house with empty eyes staring across the prairie. Out behind the farmstead there's usually a pothole or a marshy creek, and the trick is to get close enough so you can glass the water, but not so close that you scare the ducks. After we've planned our approach, whispering somewhat unnecessarily since the birds are still a quarter of a mile away, we load our guns, slip on our sunglasses, and fan out to attempt a stalk.

Once the sun gets high, the air is often warm and summery. It feels good to be wearing light shoes instead of chest waders, deerskin gloves instead of insulated mitts. About ten years ago I started wearing the same lucky hunting clothes. My warm-weather ensemble consists of a red L.L. Bean wool shirt and a buckskin vest that belonged to my father. The vest has cartridge loops on the front, in which I keep four duck loads on the right side and four goose loads on the left. Sneaking up on a pothole in that vest, tiptoeing along while exchanging whispered plans with my buddies, feeling that warm October sun overhead, I sometimes think, I couldn't be happier.

Once we get close to the water we sometimes drop to our hands and knees and crawl, or send one guy around to the far side to flush the birds. Usually, something goes wrong. Mallards are the wariest of ducks, and they have an uncanny ability to sense approaching danger. Sometimes we'll spot a wetland and slow down, and even the subtle decrease in engine noise gets the birds to explode out of the marsh grass.

I used to partner up with Paul Craft, and we polished our two-man stalking routine to the point where we didn't have to speak. We'd signal back and forth with low whistles and hand signs, like Apaches, and when we were out of sight we'd communicate telepathically. I'd crawl along on my hands and knees, nose to nose with the thistles, and pause periodically to try and get in touch with Paul. Lying there in the grass, watching a lady bug scale a stem, I'd open my head to the rhythms of the breeze, the angle of the sun, and the smell of the earth. What was Paul doing right now? Was he trying to send me a message? Was he clicking his safety off and rising on one knee to flush them?

Walking back to the truck, Paul and I would discuss the decisions we'd made and how we might have done things better. Once, after I'd ruined two stalks in a row by flushing the ducks before Paul was ready, I wondered about getting a set of cheap walkie-talkies.

"That would defeat the whole reason we're out here," said Paul. "The Indians used to be able to speak to each other with their minds, and so can we."

When you consider that ducks have a brain the size of a pea, you wouldn't think it such a challenge to outwit them. But they're wild and adaptable creatures, and they outsmart you most of the time. We're in our fifties now, but we're still learning new tricks. A couple of years ago, for example, Wynn Sweatman formed the opinion that flushed mallards "always fly upwind." As everyone knows, ducks are unpredictable, especially mallards. They might take off into the wind. But once they're airborne, they choose a random escape route— one that never seems to have any guns under it. "That's my point," Wynn argued. "They pick the safest route. If they don't see anyone upwind, they'll choose that route every time."

We tried it, and it seemed to work. At the end of the week, I tried explaining the trick to Shaun Dennehy (alias Brubaker, Bushy, Whacker, Nahanni Shaunie, etc.). Having spent much of his life in the Yukon bush, Shaun knew a lot about wildlife, and he sniffed in amusement when he heard the theory. This was while we were engaged in the usual difference of opinion, planning the last stalk of the last day. Shaun has since died of cancer, and he probably knew that this would be his last hunt. But he said he was willing to give it a try. We crept upwind of the pothole, crawling on our hands and knees, while Pete Dickson, who is a deadeye and had shot plenty of ducks already, circled downwind of the pothole to flush the birds.

187

I use a double-barreled shotgun, so for safety's sake my gun was empty as I crawled. Shaun used a pump, so he had two shells in the magazine. We'd almost reached our position when Shaun muttered, "Here they come."

The ducks had flushed early and were flying right toward us. I pulled two shells out of my vest and started loading the gun. It was like one of those paralytic moments in a bad dream. The shells weren't seated in the chambers and the gun somehow, maddeningly, wouldn't close. Precious milliseconds ticked by as my hands moved in slow motion, fumbling with the action. (Must . . . close . . . gun.)

I was still trying to close it when the ducks swept overhead. Two shots rang out, and I heard a couple of thumps as Shaun's two birds hit the ground. He limped over and picked them up—a pair of big, handsome, full-plumage drake mallards. It was the perfect conclusion to the week's hunt.

On the last night, we usually have a tailgate cookout. A few of the more conscientious individuals—Wayne Alsip and Dwight Brainerd, for example—bring wooden crates full of cookware, spices, cooking oil, and so on. This year we met down in a valley, in a stubble field next to a wooded creek, and got a fire going. Somebody handed out crackers and venison pâté, and we stood around drinking Scotch and watching our chefs prepare a massive frying pan full of potatoes, onions, bacon, and sharptail grouse.

It was cold in the late autumn darkness and we stood close to the fire, where the flames billowed in the wind. Wayne opened the door of his truck and put a Jann Arden tape in the stereo. She howled like a lonesome witch in the darkness, and the fourteen of us fell silent, staring at the fire, knowing that life doesn't get any better than this.

PETER DICKSON

JAKE MacDONALD is the author of *Houseboat Chronicles: Notes from a Life in Shield Country*, as well as five works of fiction. He is also an award-winning journalist whose writing has appeared in *Saturday Night*, *Cottage Life*, *Outdoor Canada*, *Maclean's*, and *Explore*. He lives in Winnipeg, Manitoba.